POINTS TO PONDER

Some Thoughts About How to
Live a Meaningful Life

SHALOM !

Larry Shirer
2021

Author: Larry Shirer

Title: POINTS TO PONDER:
Some Thoughts About How to Live a Meaningful Life

Subjects: Values, Virtues, Principles for Living;
How to Make Better Decisions, Be More Productive,
Search for Meaning.

ISBN: 978-1-09837-022-0
Ebook ISBN: 978-1-09837-023-7

Printed in USA

First Edition 2021

Author Website: www.larryspointstoponder.com

POINTS TO PONDER

SOME THOUGHTS ABOUT HOW TO LIVE A MEANINGFUL LIFE

TABLE OF CONTENTS

DEDICATION

This book is dedicated to my unborn granddaughter, Abby.

My hope is that she will read it someday

and find it of some value.

PREFACE - REFLECTIONS & INTENTIONS

As my eightieth birthday approaches, as I find myself eagerly anticipating the birth of my ninth grandchild, and having just completed an extensive nature exploration trip, (which involved some deep discussions), with my oldest grandson, I am struck by how different was the world in which I grew up, from the one which my 23-year-old grandson is experiencing, and how even more different will be the world my unborn grandchild will explore.

My reflections lead me to wonder if there is anything I have learned about life that is worth sharing, that is unaffected, or minimally affected, by the passage of time. I guess I am naive enough, and hopeful enough, to think the answer to that question is yes. I believe there are some values and principles that are valid, regardless of the changes in our world and how those changes impact our lives. Therefore, I have chosen to write down some thoughts about life, in the hope that they will be of benefit to my sons and daughters, grandchildren, their children, and anyone else who cares to "listen".

Socrates opined that "only an examined life is worth living". The purpose of this book is to encourage readers to examine their lives and make decisions that will make their lives <u>more</u> worthwhile, virtuous, satisfying, and meaningful.

My hope is that these observations will be useful to readers as they make decisions large and small, but primarily I share them in the hope that they will encourage readers to THINK, to figure out what is really IMPORTANT and to do what is RIGHT. I believe it is every serious thinker's responsibility to separate clarity and reason from the morass of ignorance, prejudice, dogma, and misinformation with which we are confronted daily.

I've concluded that how we answer five fundamental questions determines the quality of our lives. They provide the map for the path we choose to follow:

- Who do I choose to be?
- How do I choose to see the world?
- How do I choose to live my life?
- What might I to do improve my life?
- What's it all about?

By design or default we all make these choices. They are inescapable. The "right" answers to these questions are not the same for everyone, but there are principles and values, which if applied, make some choices more effective than others.

Life poses many problems. With those we must learn to cope. Life also offers goodness, beauty, hope and truth. Of these, we should learn to be aware and to appreciate.

I offer many suggestions for getting control of one's life, and living a life that is satisfying and meaningful. Please understand that I am not trying to tell anyone what to do, with these general exceptions: I urge everyone to THINK, to DECIDE, to DO. I am convinced that following a proactive agenda is superior to being reactive or doing nothing at all.

I offer some ideas regarding what to THINK about. To be sure, my list is not all inclusive. I offer some suggestions about how to decide and what to do. The deciding and doing are up to you. My conclusions may not all be accurate. My suggestions may not be appropriate. You may decide differently. That is ok. What is important is that you seriously think about the issues raised and decide what makes sense for you, in light of your carefully considered values, principles, morals, ethics and goals.

I like to think of myself as a "Seeker of Truth". I have a burning desire to know the truth, the way "things really are". Having said that, I understand no one can ever possess all truth, or only the truth. Life is too complicated for that. Truth can only be pursued. But that in no way diminishes the value of the search. The more I learn, the more I reflect, the closer I get to reality. For me, reality is important. What I share here is what I have come to believe about the truth regarding the subjects addressed. There is no guarantee that what you read here is THE TRUTH. It represents what <u>I think</u> is true. What is the truth for you, you must decide for yourself.

Part of what I share is background information and opinion. In some cases, my suggestions may represent what I have learned about what should be done, what I learned by doing the wrong things, or doing things incorrectly. I offer them in the hope that you will not make the same mistakes that I have made.

I make no claim that all of this material is original. I have borrowed extensively from the wisdom of others. Sometimes I give credit and use quotation marks. Sometimes I paraphrase what I have learned from reading or hearing, and/or I extrapolate from what I have read, heard or experienced.

As you will see in this text, I am fond of quotations and "old" adages that resonate with truth and meaning. The one that I lately find myself relating to more and more is:

"Too Soon Old, Too Late Smart"

I hope you will find these ramblings of some value.

Larry Shirer

We won't find the meaning of life by accumulating lots of money, stuff, social status, or fame. Meaning is found by living a life of love and respect for self, others and the world in which we live, by making a difference for good in the lives of others, by always acting with integrity, by accepting our responsibilities and striving for positive personal achievements. We determine the meaning of our lives by who we are and what we do.

PART I. WHO DO I CHOOSE TO BE?

The development of our true nature, our essence, is fundamental and very important. It determines our futures. When we examine who we are, we may not be happy with what we find. We may find imperfections. That is inevitable. It is critical to understand that we are not irrevocably locked into the condition created by our personal history and our circumstances. We all have the freedom and ability to learn and grow, to become, if not the ideal, at least closer to, the person we would like to be. By design or default, we daily create the persons we will be from that day forth.

CHOICES

Choices matter! Individual decisions, the choices we make, literally determine the course and quality of our lives. Our most important choices involve who we chose to be as persons. Who we are, what we do, our mental and emotional state, who and what we will become, all depend largely upon the <u>decisions</u> we make. Our happiness, success, health, achievements, morality and the extent to which our lives have meaning are determined primarily by the quality of our decisions. Aristotle, a respected Greek philosopher, observed long ago that "we become what we are as persons by the decisions that we make." That truth hasn't changed. The quality of our lives is determined by the decisions we make.

I found the following on a plaque in a gift shop. I bought the plaque and mounted it along my "Ponder Path" in the woods behind our home, to remind me daily of what is important and that I am responsible for my life:

LIVE THE LIFE YOU'VE
ALWAYS DREAMED OF.
BE FEARLESS IN THE FACE OF ADVERSITY.
RECOGNIZE THE BEAUTY
THAT SURROUNDS YOU.
NEVER STOP LEARNING.
REMEMBER WHERE YOU
CAME FROM, BUT DON'T
LOSE SIGHT OF WHERE
YOU ARE GOING.
USE YOUR IMAGINATION.
**THIS LIFE IS YOURS
TO CREATE.**

We make lots of decisions. The only thing we do more than make decisions is breathe. We make hundreds of decisions every day. Many are not earth shaking – what should I wear today? Which cereal should I have for breakfast? Some are life-changing - What career should I pursue? Should I go into debt to attend college? Is she/he the right spouse for me? Should I "try" addictive substances? Unfortunately, other than perhaps "fretting" a little more, we often approach important decisions much like we do the minor ones.

Decisions drive everything. Decisions determine whether our nation goes to war and sends our young people off to fight and die. Decisions determine whether our economy grows or stagnates. Decisions determine whether our planet can continue to support life as we know it. Our fate is determined by our personal decisions, by the decisions of elected officials, bureaucrats, corporate executives and others in positions of influence. The choices we make, when we vote at the ballot box, when we express our opinions with our voices, with our feet and with our spending money, all matter. The future of our economy, our country, and our planet will be determined by the quality of individual and collective human decisions.

We have access to huge amounts of information and many options. We are required to choose: values, goals and objectives, careers, where to reside, a spouse, (or not to have one), a worldview, what personal philosophy and religion to embrace, (or to embrace none), how to relate to people, and more. We are bombarded with the need to make choices. How well we cope depends on how clearly we think.

Occasionally factors and events beyond our control significantly impact our lives. Things happen to us. But, to a much greater extent than we often admit, we mold our lives and control our future through the decisions we make. Other people make decisions that affect us, but we can always choose our response, and thus determine what happens next.

Although decision making is among the most frequent things we do and certainly among the **most important things we do**, we are not typically taught how to do it, nor do most of us consciously make an effort to learn to do it. We are presumably supposed to learn decision making by observation or through experience. Observing the results of others' decisions can be helpful, but observation, by itself, does not work well for learning to make decisions. And while experience, "the school of hard knocks", can provide useful lessons, as the sole method of learning it is very inefficient and often painful.

Important decisions, those that have significant ramifications for us and for others, warrant focused time and effort. Decision making is a <u>critical life skill</u>. Fortunately, it's a skill that can be learned and improved. We can learn to be better decision makers. Like learning to drive a car, it can be awkward at first, but we get more proficient with practice. To make better decisions, one has to *want* to learn and to grow in proficiency.

Not all decisions are of equal importance. Some influence our lives more than others. Decisions made today may impact our lives for years down the road. Choosing the wrong <u>vacation</u> may have minimal impact in the long run. Choosing the wrong <u>vocation</u> can make one's life miserable. Evaluating the importance of decisions is critical.

Not all decisions are of a "yes or no" or "black or white" type. Most important decisions involve shades of gray. Most must be made with less than all the information that could be relevant. Many must be made under time and/or other pressures. Some involve tradeoffs between conflicting objectives and rules. In spite of all these obstacles, learning to make the best choices, with the information and time available, is possible and can be very rewarding.

Making wise decisions involves asking oneself a lot of fundamental questions, and honestly attempting to seek truthful and useful answers to those questions.

We can learn to make better decisions by: becoming more aware of their impact on our lives, taking responsibility for our decisions, consciously committing to improving them, developing a truthful and realistic understanding of the world within which we make decisions and employing an effective decision making <u>process</u>.

While the typical purpose of decision making is to produce positive results, outcomes are often uncertain. Even with the careful application of the best process, there is no guarantee the results of a given decision will be positive. Good decisions can have negative consequences and poor decisions, by chance or luck, can be followed by great results. An evaluation of whether a decision was "good" or "bad" should relate, not just to the results, but to <u>how</u> the choice was made. Following an effective process will, in the long run, produce better results than knee jerk reactions and hap-hazard approaches.

Understand that no one makes <u>only</u> good decisions. Our objective should be, not to make *"perfect"* decisions every time, but to <u>make *"better"* decisions more often</u>, to increase the odds that the consequences will be positive. Following a systematic, logical process and consciously attempting to think rationally can help significantly.

An effective process + wisdom = better decisions. Better decisions = a better quality of life.

Making important decisions can be tough and the consequences serious. Most of our more serious life problems are the result of poor decisions. Our prisons are full of people who made poor choices.

Many of our poor decisions are the result of not understanding *how* to make effective decisions. The quality of our decisions is determined not only by *what* we decide, but to a great extent by *how* we decide. The process is important. Using an effective process will not make tough decisions easy, but it will provide the assurance that we have given the issue our best effort and will increase the probability of a successful outcome. We will address the decision-making process in the subsequent Part V.

<u>PRINCIPLES</u>

A life of meaning and satisfaction is based, not on material wealth, but on living a life aligned with the right principles. Principles are not rules developed by a committee, but are derived from the experiences of what has worked best for our species. They represent the time and experience tested collective wisdom of humankind. Examples include: integrity, justice, compassion, accepting responsibility, generosity, self-control, meeting commitments, respect, love, and service.

VALUES

Core principles are based upon sound values. Values are those standards and qualities we deem to have inherent worth and which we consider deeply important. Making good decisions involves more than weighing facts and figures. The best decisions are not necessarily those which are the easiest, the most convenient, or the most personally beneficial. Choices which are effective and with which we can live comfortably, are choices consistent with our core values. Decisions drive behavior. If our behavior is not consistent with our values, we will feel dissatisfied with the results, uncomfortable, and out of sync with the world. When our actions are consistent with our values, we are much more likely to achieve positive outcomes and be more satisfied with our choices.

> "Carefully watch your thoughts, for they become your words. Manage and watch your words, for they become your actions. Consider and judge your actions, for they become your habits. Acknowledge and watch your habits, for they become your values. Understand and embrace your values, for they become your destiny."
> Mahatma Gandhi

Values are the foundation of character. Character determines self-respect and the respect with which we are regarded by others. Choosing personal values are some of the most important decisions we ever make. They determine the kind of person we become. Once established, they should serve as guides for making other important decisions. Our values should provide an internal compass that guides the direction of our life journeys. With every decision we make, we are writing the stories of our lives. We should strive to make our stories ones of which we can be proud and which have meaning.

In thinking about which values are important, we should consider the following questions:

- How do I define right and wrong?
- What do I consider to be my moral absolutes?
- How do I define ethics in dealing with people?
- What do I consider to be my basic personal responsibilities
- What are the qualities I admire about people I respect?
- What makes me feel fulfilled and proud?
- What values were involved in decisions I regret?

Values imbue our lives with meaning. They define who we are and who we want to be. They often involve making choices about what is right and wrong and what is the responsible thing to do under the circumstances. To determine if a decision is "right", <u>we should test possible choices against our values</u>. To test a decision against our values, we must, of course, have previously considered and defined our ethical and moral standards and what core values are really important to us. That requires careful thought and is something that should be done with deliberation and great care, before we are faced with the pressure of making important decisions. By deciding *now* what is important, we will be better prepared to <u>align our actions with our values</u> in times of crisis or change.

Decisions about personal values deserve and require careful deliberation. To facilitate thinking about what values are important to you, complete the following exercise:

1. The following is a list of 75 common personal values cited by persons who were asked about such things. Add to the list any others you believe important and combine any two or more you consider similar enough to be considered as one.

Accountability	Accuracy	Status
Tenacity	Self Confidence	Commitment to Family
Achievement	Goodness	Fun
Wealth	Gratitude	Financial Security
Compassion	Ambition	Integrity
Balance / Harmony	Work Ethic	Leisure
Calmness	Assertiveness	Physical Safety
Commitment	Belonging	Independence
Freedom	Control	Happiness
Dependability	Cooperation	Contentment
Fairness	Spirituality	Physical Fitness
Friendship	Creativity	Personal Growth
Faith	Health	Serenity
Generosity	Serving Others	Thoughtfulness
Respect	Stability	Structure
Competitiveness	Challenge	Logic
Consistency	Love	Reliability
Excitement	Dependability	Being Organized
Fame	Perseverance	Learning / Education
Contribution	Intelligence	Inclusiveness / Diversity
Courtesy	Respect for Nature	Artistic Expression
Creativity	Humility	Empathy
Decisiveness	Self-Control	Justice
Determination	Being Responsible	Loyalty
Expertise	Success	Seeking Truth

2. From your modified list, check or circle the 10-12 you consider most important.

3. For each of the 10-12 selected, write down a definition of what the term means to you. Writing the definitions forces you to really think about what the concepts mean and why they are important. The following are examples of such definitions:

- Honesty & Integrity – To be honest is to be real, genuine, authentic, to deal equitably with others, to not take things to which you have no right and to always tell the truth.
- Responsibility – Responsible people are those who take charge of themselves and their conduct. Ultimately, we are responsible for the kinds of persons we have made of ourselves. Being responsible means meeting commitments and being accountable for our actions.
- Work Ethic – Work is expending energy for the sake of accomplishing something or achieving something. It is doing something worthwhile that one can take pride in doing well. Work should be viewed as something positive, something of value, not punishment or drudgery. The opposite of work is not play or having fun, but idleness, not investing ourselves in anything, wasting time.

4. Review and evaluate your list.
   a. Would acting in accordance with these values make you feel good about yourself?
   b. Are these really your values or values that someone told you that you should have?
   c. Would you be proud to share these values with someone you admire and respect?

d. Would you be willing to stick with and defend these values in situations where others might disagree with or attack them?

5. Select the 5-7 you think most important, with their definitions. Keep this short list in your wallet or purse.

6. When deliberating about a decision, test your short list of choices against this list of values to determine how consistent each possible solution is with your core values.

This exercise takes time and careful consideration, but is well worth the effort. Just conscientiously completing the exercise will improve the quality of your decisions, because it forces you to think about what is important to you.

Identifying, understanding and applying core values is an important part of an effective decision making strategy. Becoming more aware of how critical values are in your life and applying them to the decisions you make will be useful for making choices that are effective, and about which you can feel confident.

> "It is time to return to core values, time to get back to basics, to self-discipline and respect for the law, to consideration for others, to accepting responsibility for yourself and your family-and not shuffling it off on other people or the state."
> John Major

Choose your core values, principles and ideals well. Express them through everything you do. The gift of free will is that we can choose our behaviors, we can choose to be evil or choose to be good. Figure out what is fundamental to who you want to be. Choose a course that results in peace of mind and self-respect. Do not compromise on the basics, but be very flexible about everything else.

> "Values are principles and ideas that bring meaning to the seemingly mundane experience of life. A meaningful life that ultimately brings happiness and pride requires you to respond to temptation, as well as challenges, with honor, dignity and courage."
> Laura Schlessinger

SELF KNOWLEDGE

How we see ourselves matters. Our perceptions of self can severely limit who we are and who we can become, or can unchain and inspire us to be what we decide to be.

> "Knowing others is intelligence.
> Knowing yourself is true wisdom.
> Mastering others is strength.
> Mastering yourself is true power."
> The Tao Te Ching

The ways of thinking about decision making outlined herein encourage you to consider who you are and who you want to be, to ponder your values and your priorities, to determine what gives your life meaning and what gives you particular satisfaction. If you have pet peeves, if you tend to have particular fears, acknowledge them and reflect on how they might be affecting your choices. All these factors are elements of self-knowledge which impact decision making.

> "It takes courage to grow up and become who you really are."
> E.E. Cummings

The more clearly we understand our strengths and weaknesses, our values and what we want from life, the more effective our choices will be. Know what you want and don't want. When gathering information for making decisions, don't overlook relevant information about the decision <u>maker</u> (you). Get to know yourself. If you are dissatisfied with what you find, think about the qualities you admire in people you respect most, (living or dead). Reflect on those qualities and emulate them.

> "I found power in accepting the truth of who I am. It may not be a truth that others can accept, but I cannot live any other way. How would it be to live a lie every minute of your life?"
> Alison Goodman

The essence of rationality is respect for the facts of reality. The fact is, we have needs, motives, emotions, beliefs, mental states, goals, ambitions, and feelings. To function effectively, we need to be conscious of both external and internal realities. We should make self-awareness a conscious element of our decision-making process.

Socrates said, "The unexamined life is not worth living." It follows then that the thoroughly examined life, the life focused on meaning, is <u>well</u> worth living.

Consider the standards by which you measure the effectiveness of your decisions. Make sure they are realistic and relevant. Self-knowledge can help you achieve your goals. Make sure those goals are worthy, are yours, not someone else's, and not what you think society wants you to be.

We all have fears. Fear is not all bad. Some fears help keep us alive. Fears that facilitate self-preservation are functional. Fears of the unknown are often irrational and crippling. Seeking positive, but unfamiliar, new relationships and experiences can help us grow and learn. Fears rooted in selfishness distort reality. Fears driven by motives of greed, control and insecurity are dysfunctional. They impede effective decision making. Identify and categorize your fears and examine them for validity.

> "Courage is resistance to fear, mastery of fear - not absence of fear."
> Mark Twain

Making the right decision sometimes takes courage. We develop courage by facing our fears, examining their causes and rationality, and doing what is right in spite of them.

Acquiring the skill to choose our attitudes, to choose our thoughts and to choose what actions we take may be the most critical skills we can develop. Self–knowledge is fundamental to developing those skills. Know thyself.

> "Integrity is congruence between what you know, what you profess, and what you do."
> Nathaniel Branden

> "I learned that courage was not the absence of fear, but the triumph over it. The brave man is not he who does not feel afraid, but he who conquers that fear."
> Nelson Mandela

We must be very careful of "*labels*" we assign to ourselves or that are affixed to us by others. If we see ourselves as "*poor at math*", we will not do well in math. If we see ourselves as "*dishonest*", we are likely to steal. If we see ourselves as "*disabled*", we will act out our perception of what disabled means. If we see ourselves as "*a victim of a broken home*", we will act like a victim. If we <u>believe</u> labels assigned by others: *lazy, dumb, clumsy*, we are likely to act as labeled. If we see ourselves as capable, caring and worthy, we are much more likely to achieve. We are not our symptoms, our real or imagined defects. We can choose not to be prisoners of our history, our environment, our circumstances or the perceptions of others.

CHARACTER

Character development, the transition from a preoccupation with self, to consciousness of and caring for others, is an important element of personal growth. Our characters define who we are as persons. Character determines how we respond to the events and circumstances in our lives. How we respond determines the results of those encounters.

> "What lies behind us and what lies before us are small matters compared to what lies within us."
> Oliver Wendell Holmes

One's worth as an individual is determined by character, not by titles, educational degrees, possessions or wealth. Character is influenced by genes, experiences, examples and education, but is largely determined by judgement, discretion and personal choices. Character is malleable, we get to choose which traits we want to develop and emphasize. Our "self" is elastic. We can mold it if we so choose. A person of "strong" character is one who is moral and ethical, does what is right in spite of personal gain or hardship, cares about people and can be trusted.

Character defines who we are. In the final analysis, who we <u>are</u> determines the worth, the effectiveness, of our lives, and communicates what we value much more eloquently than anything we say. Our character is defined by the **principles** by which we conduct our lives. Many generations of multiple cultures have demonstrated that there are basic principles for effective living, and that people can be truly successful and happy only if they learn to integrate those principles into their basic characters. The shaping of character is based upon the fundamental idea that there are certain principles that govern human decency and effectiveness, natural laws in the human dimension that are just as real as natural laws in the physical dimension, (such as the law of gravity). These principles and values are the foundation on which we should each erect the structure of our character:

Morality & Ethics - Not all decisions involve moral choices. Choosing the restaurant at which to have lunch is morally neutral. Others, such as decisions about whether to lie, cheat or steal, can have profound consequences. Those that force us to consider what is *"right and wrong"* can be challenging. There is more to determining if a decision is the *"right"* one, than deciding that it solves the problem, resolves the issue or maximizes personal benefit. To be *"right"*, a decision must not only meet our objectives, but also be moral and ethical.

> "So, I think ethics is a broader thing that's less focused on prohibitions and is more about looking at principles, questions and ideas about how to live your life".
> Peter Singer

Morality is about how we treat people. Right decisions are those that resolve our issues, while demonstrating respect for peoples' rights and concern for peoples' needs. "Right" decisions treat people fairly and with decency.

The Buddha taught that one of the steps on the "Right Path" is the practice of "Right Action". He distinguished between right actions and right results. We cannot always control results. We can only choose the best action given the best motives and what we know. The Right Actions are those that help others and support a peaceful and honorable life.

We should not confuse morality with pleasing people. Doing the right thing does not always please everyone involved. People sometimes get very upset and angry with us for doing what is in their best interests, as anyone who has reared children can attest.

There are lots of moral rules. Some people embrace more rules than do others, especially rules for other people. Not all moral rules are created equal. There are some, just a few, which we should <u>almost</u> always follow. One involves justice. We should strive to always be fair to all concerned. Another involves compassion. We should demonstrate concern for, and strive to help, people who need us. A third involves human dignity. We should respect the right to "life, liberty and the pursuit of happiness" for all individuals. Other important moral rules involve honesty and integrity. We should keep promises, tell the truth and respect the property rights of others. The best decisions are those that reflect compassion, equity and integrity.

Both rules and results matter. Achieving objectives and solving problems matter. But, if we focus only on personal ends, we may wreak havoc with the lives of others. Focusing only on rules is not always optimal.

> "Learn and obey the rules very well, so you will know how to break them properly."
> The Dalai Lama

Sometimes the end does justify the means. Although it's often not easy, our task is to find the right balance between rules and results.

> "Never let your sense of morals prevent you from doing what is right."
> Isaac Asimov

As a general rule, most agree that doing what results in the greatest "*good*" for the greatest number is usually a wise choice. But, exceptions are easy to identify. It is questionable to contend that we should <u>always</u> follow rules. Who among us would refrain from stealing food if that was the only available option for feeding our starving child? Who would refrain from doing bodily harm to an attacker bent upon killing a loved one?

> "Ethics is knowing the difference between what you have a right to do and what is right to do."
> Potter Stewart

Making moral decisions is a process that develops one's conscience. Small decisions become a pattern. Most people don't suddenly decide that they will become thieves, cheaters or liars. They look back one day and discover that they have become thieves, cheaters or liars. We must pay attention to the *pattern* of our moral decisions. Little choices add up to define who we are. We don't have to be perfect, but it is important that we be "*good*".

Most of us have been trapped in what we consider to be situations "*between a rock and a hard place*". Things are not always black or white. Choosing between right and wrong can be difficult. Consider both rules and consequences. Recognize that moral and ethical rules are useful, applicable most of the time, but not absolute. We should think through our moral obligations and try our best to do what's right.

> "Compassion is the basis of morality."
> Arthur Schopenhaur

It is important to examine the "*why*" of our choices. We must be careful about confusing "*wants*" and "*oughts*". We should pay more attention to what is right than to what we want.

> "Happiness is in many things. It's in love. It's in sharing. But most of all it's in being at peace with yourself knowing that you are making the effort, the full effort, to do what is right."
> John Wooden

Honesty/Integrity - connotes not cheating, lying or stealing. Honesty is the foundation for trust, which is essential to cooperation and interpersonal relationships.

> "I hope I shall possess firmness and virtue enough to maintain what I consider the most enviable of all titles, the character of an honest man."
> George Washington

True/Truth – We typically think of true as the opposite of false and truth as the opposite of a lie. While these understandings are accurate, they are not complete. The concepts are multi-dimensional. Certainly, we should speak only the truth. What we say reflects who we are. Lying is destructive to relationships. Statements, contentions, facts cannot be both true and false, as those of us who have taken true/false quizzes in school can attest. But there's more to the concepts:

- True can mean straight, or perfectly square, as in a carpenter constructing a door frame so that the door will open and close properly. A carpenter may use a "plumb bob" or a "square" to determine what is "*true*'. It is unfortunate that we don't have such a tool for telling us if what we hear and read is "*true*".
- True can mean "*real*", as in; he is a "*true*" friend.
- True can mean "*exemplary*", as in: he is a "*true*" gentleman.
- True can mean "*demonstrable*", as in: ice melts at temperatures above 32 degrees F.
- True can mean "*actual*" as opposed to imaginary, as in; "*true story*" publications.
- True can mean "*valuable*", "*meaningful*" or "*useful*" when referring to the message in a story that is not necessarily factual.

Black Elk, a famous and oft quoted Sioux Medicine Man, when commenting upon one of the myths of his people, stated: "…this they tell, and whether it happened or not, I do not know, but if you think about it, you will see that it is true."

All of these dimensions of truth have relevance to how we live our lives. Living truthfully means not telling lies, but much more. It means being true to who we want to be and what we want to do. We should be true, real, to others, but more importantly, true to ourselves, true to our values and to what we "know" as right.

> "I prefer to be true to myself, even at the hazard of incurring the ridicule of others, rather than be false, and to incur my own abhorrence."
> William Douglass

We can never know all truth or the whole truth. Nevertheless, we should seek truth. The value is in the search, the striving, and in the satisfaction of knowing you have found a piece of it.

Believing does not make things true, nor does denying that something is true make it false. Some things, like gravity, are just naturally true, whether we believe them or not. Denying that gravity exists does not cause us to fly off the earth. Some things are not true, and never will be, no matter how earnestly we want them to be true.

What is true for us may change. The world changes. We change. What was true for us at age ten is not the same as what is true for us at age 80. That is not a bad thing. It is inevitable. We've had more experiences, learned more. Our circumstances have changed.

We face a particular challenge today. We are bombarded daily by information, and conclusions based upon that information, from our smartphones, computers, televisions, newspapers and magazines (at least for those of us who still read newspapers and magazines). We hear and read a lot about "fake news". (During World War II, it was labeled propaganda). A lot of the information is contradictory. How can we possibly decide what is *"true"*? How should we test what we hear and read?

There are no concrete answers to those questions. One can only apply informed, rational judgement. Asking the following questions and thinking about the answers may be useful:

- Are the information and conclusions consistent with what I think I know about the subject?
- Is it logical? Do the conclusions reasonably follow from the premises?
- Is the information consistent with my experience?
- Is the source reliable? Have the information and conclusions offered by this source in the past been accurate?
- How can I cross check the information with other sources? How does it compare?
- What are the logical consequences of believing the information and "buying" the conclusions?
- Are believing and buying consistent with my values and principles?

We must think it through.

Respect for Human Dignity - All persons have intrinsic worth and certain "unalienable rights", which we must honor if we expect to enjoy those same rights.

Compassion - People matter. We should be ever aware of the impact of our actions, words and decisions on others. Almost all our decisions affect other people. We should treat people with dignity and respect. Things are to be used, *people* are to be loved. Loving things and using people inevitably lead to poor consequences. Part of our reason for being is to help lighten the burdens of others.

Kindness – The attribute of kindness encompasses being attentive, considerate, generous, empathetic and friendly. It involves listening to and helping others. It means celebrating the successes of others and sharing their woes. It is an interpersonal skill that engenders trust and strengthens relationships. It means showing others, in a multitude of little ways, that we care.

> "Unexpected kindness is the most powerful, least costly, and most underrated agent of human change."
> Bob Kerry

> "Constant kindness can accomplish much. As the sun makes ice to melt, kindness causes misunderstanding, mistrust and hostility to evaporate."
> Albert Schweitzer

This may seem obvious, but think about it. We become kind persons by doing kind things.

Responsibility - No matter how good or bad our decisions, we are responsible for the consequences. We are responsible for our thoughts, beliefs, values, words, choices and actions. We are responsible for how we treat other people, for keeping our promises, for our lives and personal well-being. Blaming others or finding excuses does not change that reality. Recognizing and accepting personal responsibility will motivate us to make better decisions.

Being responsible requires self-discipline and effective time management. It means being conscientious, mindful, accountable and dependable. We should be particularly conscious of what we say, for words can wound deeper than a knife. We must accept that we have control. If we don't do something, nothing is going to get better. We must choose not to be victims. We should not, as many do, blame our circumstances on someone else's actions or on the "system". Accepting responsibility is the first step to finding solutions.

> "The moment you accept responsibility for EVERYTHING in your life is the moment you gain the power to change ANYTHING in your life."
> Hal Elrod

We should avoid falling into the trap of blaming someone or circumstances for our actions, as in: "I wouldn't have done that if she hadn't ....., or "he (or the devil) made me do it." We shouldn't offer lame excuses: "I felt hurt, so I ...", "I felt angry, so I ....", "I felt afraid, so I ...". "I couldn't help it." We have choices about how we respond to circumstances and the actions of others. We are responsible for our feelings and our actions.

We must be pro-active, avoiding the mindset "Why doesn't someone do something?" Instead we should ask "What should I do?" Then do something.

We need to forego any feelings of entitlement. A journalist for *TIME MAGAZINE* characterized this "entitlement" attitude, of far too many, as follows: "If I want it, I need it. If I need it, I have a right to it. If I have a right to it, someone owes it to me...". The concept of accepting responsibility is contrary to the idea of entitlement.

The respect and trust of persons who we respect and trust are valuable assets. We earn that respect and trust by being competent and accountable and by accepting responsibility for our actions.

We are each responsible for who we are, what we do, what we say, how we treat people and how we live our lives. We are responsible for the consequences of our decisions. Accept personal responsibility.

> "People are always blaming their circumstances for what they are. I don't believe in circumstances. The people who get on in this world are the people who get up and look for the circumstances they want, and if they can't find them, make them."
>
> George Bernard Shaw

In his book, *TAKING RESPONSIBILITY*, PhD Psychologist Nathaniel Branden suggests we start each day with two questions: "What's good in my life? and What needs to be done? The first question keeps us focused on the positives. The second reminds us that our life and well-being are our own responsibility and keeps us proactive."

Conscientiousness - Studies have shown that one trait shared by those of high achievement and happiness is conscientiousness.

> "Conscientiousness is emerging as one of the primary determinants of successful functioning across the lifespan."
>
> Paul Tough

Literally, being conscientious means following one's conscience, doing what is right. Developing a sound value system and living those values is important. Conscientiousness also means more. Being conscientious means being dependable, doing what we say we will do and being there for others, demonstrating that others can count on us. Being conscientious means being aware of, and responsive to, the needs of others.

> "Good luck is the willing handmaiden of an upright character and the conscientious observance of duty".
>
> James Russell Lowell

Being conscientious also means caring about the quality of what one does. We do not have to be perfect or do things perfectly, but setting high standards and striving to meet them leads to greater satisfaction and achievement and earns the respect of others.

Be conscientious. It will help you fulfill your responsibilities to others and enhance how you feel about yourself and what you do.

> "Being conscientious is like brushing your teeth. It prevents problems."
> Brent Roberts

Self-Control - Demonstrating self-control involves choosing thoughtful, rational responses to external stimuli, responses which are consistent with one's values and goals. It is the process of avoiding compulsive, self-destructive reactions to temptations, threats, addictions or provocations. Permitting negative emotions to influence decisions can have devastating effects. Self-control is about mastering one's life rather than being slave to one's emotions. It is not about taking all the fun out of life. It is about making intelligent choices. Self-control is a combination of will, commitment, courage and taking responsibility for one's actions. It is also a concept of free will and choice. We have to choose to exercise it.

> "If you are not in control of your thoughts, then you are not in control of yourself. Without self-control, you have no real power, regardless of whatever else you accomplish. If you are not aware of the thoughts that you are thinking, then you are a rider with no reins, with no power over where you are going. You cannot control what you are not aware of. Awareness must come first."
> Thomas M. Steiner

Impulsive, irrational behaviors can result in poor decisions that: harm personal heath and well-being, can impair personal effectiveness and can damage relationships.

> "Self-control is the chief element in self-respect, and self-respect is the chief element in courage."
> Thucydides

Developing self-control involves awareness, the understanding that we can choose our emotions and thoughts, and the identification of our personal "hot buttons" -- stimuli that typically set off "automatic", personal and/or relationship damaging, emotional responses.

To establish control we should:

1. Identify personal issues/instances over which we wish to exert more effective control.
2. Identify the damaging, typical reactions to which we are prone and the emotions that drive them.
3. Make a decision to develop more effective responses.
4. Tell ourselves: "I am in control of my thoughts, emotions and reactions, I am in charge of my behavior".
5. Visualize how you would like to calmly and rationally deal with the issue.
6. Recognize the volatile issues when they come up and practice our planned responses.

The good news is that, like a muscle, self-control gets stronger with regular exercise. The important thing is to practice overriding damaging, habitual ways of doing things and exerting deliberate control over our actions.

> "Respond intelligently, even to unintelligent treatment."
> Lao-tsu

> "Never respond to an angry person with a fiery comeback, even if he deserves it. Don't allow his anger to become your anger."
>
> Bohdi Sanders

Fairness/Justice - Fairness is the principle upon which our whole system of justice is based and the foundation for our understanding of what is "right". Justice is the principle upon which right relationships are built. Treat others fairly.

Quality/Excellence - Whatever we do, we should do it well.

Do No Harm – The most basic principle of all is that of not harming others. It includes not controlling or manipulating others, nor trying to manage their affairs.

Meet Commitments – Demonstrating that we always do what we say we will do earns us the trust and respect of others and a clear conscience. Failing to meet commitments betrays others and ourselves.

> "Resolve to perform what you ought; perform without fail what you resolve."
>
> Benjamin Franklin

Courage - Courage is not the absence of fear. Demonstrating courage means doing what is right regardless of criticism, personal hardship, or popular opinion. Demonstrating courage includes confronting and attempting to correct injustice and unfairness.

> "Keep strong, if possible. In any case, keep cool. Have unlimited patience. Never corner an opponent, and always assist him to save face. Put yourself in his shoes – so as to see things through his eyes. Avoid self-righteousness like the devil – nothing is so self-blinding.
>
> B. H. Liddell Hart

Understand that strong character is not the result of instant transformation. It is the result of the multitude of struggles that we wage in our minds between selfishness and selflessness, good and evil, greed and benevolence. We become more disciplined, considerate and responsible through thousands of small acts of generosity, service, self-control and compassion.

These principles are guidelines for human conduct that have been proven to have enduring, intrinsic value. Integrating them into our characters will make our lives richer, more effective and more satisfying. We should practice them, make them habits, and pass them on. Of all the variables that determine how we live our lives, character matters most. Character is the bedrock that enables us to deal effectively with the circumstances and challenges of life. Mold it well and it will serve you well.

PART II. HOW DO I CHOOSE TO SEE THE WORLD?

Our perceptions of how the world functions and what is important, particularly our perceptions about people, affect the decisions we make and our satisfaction with life. Someone who views people as basically "good" and of inherent worth will make different decisions than one who views people as inherently "evil" and out to take advantage of others. The more accurate one's worldview, the closer it aligns with reality, the better one's decisions will be and the more stable one's life will be. There are many facets to a personal worldview. The concept includes one's knowledge, philosophy, attitudes, principles, values, emotions, morality, ethics, biases and more.

The following are observations about some of the more important elements of a worldview. These elements should be given serious thought, because they have a huge impact on choices, life outcomes and one's satisfaction with life.

POSITIVE or NEGATIVE

Seeing a glass as half full instead of half empty is more than a platitude. It indicates how we see the world, and how we see the world affects the way we live your lives.

> "If you concentrate on finding whatever is good in every situation, you will discover that your life will suddenly be filled with gratitude, a feeling that nurtures the soul."
>
> Rabbi Harold Kushner

"Positive Thinking" has gotten a lot of ink since Norman Vincent Peale published his book on the subject, *The Power of Positive Thinking*, in 1952. The concept is dismissed by some as unrealistically "looking at the world through rose colored glasses" and ignoring the negative aspects of life. That is unfortunate because it really connotes dealing with life's challenges with a positive attitude. It means trying to see the good in other people, considering yourself and your capabilities as worthy and attempting to make the best of bad situations.

Studies have shown that people with positive attitudes toward life are typically healthier and happier than those with negative attitudes. These are real benefits, and recent research indicates there are also positive implications for decision making.

Psychological research at the University of North Carolina demonstrated that experiencing positive thoughts and emotions enabled participants to visualize and articulate more possibilities and alternatives than did those with negative thoughts and emotions. The same research also indicates that a positive attitude helps one build skill sets (like decision making and problem-solving), that have long range benefits. This has implications for the process of searching for alternatives and options when making decisions.

A positive attitude doesn't happen by chance. It requires a decision. A positive mindset makes you feel better and helps you make better choices. Think Positively!

SCARCITY or ABUNDANCE

The concepts of Scarcity and Abundance mindsets were, if not coined, at least widely publicized by Stephen Covey in his best-selling book *THE 7 HABITS OF HIGHLY EFFECTIVE PEOPLE.* Covey wrote:

> "Most people are deeply scripted in what I call the Scarcity Mentality. They see life as having only so much, as though there was only one pie out there, and if someone else were to get a big piece of the pie, it would

mean less for everybody else. The Scarcity Mentality is a zero-sum paradigm of life."

Those with a Scarcity Mindset are convinced there is simply not enough to go around. Their perception is that if they are to get "more", they have to take it away from someone else. If someone else gets "more", it means there is "less" for them. The scarcity mindset focuses on the short term and ignores the long term. It fosters selfishness and competitiveness rather than collaboration. It creates feelings of jealousy and sadness at another's success or gain.

About the Abundance Mindset, Covey wrote:

> "The Abundance Mindset, on the other hand, flows from a deep inner sense of personal worth and security. It is the paradigm that there is plenty out there and enough to spare for everybody. It results in the sharing of prestige, of recognition, of profits, of decision making. It opens possibilities, options, alternatives and creativity."

Peter Diamandis and Steven Kotler in their book, appropriately titled *ABUNDANCE,* convincingly contend the Scarcity Mentality is not only fallacious, but effectively stifles creativity, as well as the ability to find solutions to significant world problems. It is a self-fulfilling mindset. Believing: the "hole is too deep to climb out of, the problems are too big to solve, the trends are worsening instead of improving", cause many to give up hope. Thus these beliefs get in the way of finding effective solutions. They foster an attitude of "why should I care, the world is going to hell anyway".

The authors point out that because we are "hard wired" to be alert to threats, and respond instinctively to them, (a condition necessary for the survival of our ancestors), and because we are constantly bombarded with "bad news" (bad news sells papers and air time), we have a negative cognitive bias – we tend to give more weight to negative information and experiences than positive ones. "The inability of people to see the positive trends through the sea of bad news – that may be the biggest stumbling block on the road toward abundance."

Diamandis and Kotler further argue the world's major problems are solvable. What it takes is a different way of framing the issues and visualizing solutions.

Resolve to be a part of the solution, not a part of the problem. Think WIN/WIN! Think ABUNDANCE!

WHO IS IN CONTROL?

You can choose to view yourself as a helpless <u>victim</u> of circumstances and the whims of others, or as <u>master</u> of your fate. There is a lot of truth to the old adage that "If it is to be, it is up to me". Lots of research indicates that those who take personal responsibility for their lives are more successful and happier than those who attribute their life consequences to external forces.

The findings of noted clinical psychologist Julian Rotter indicate that *where* one perceives oneself on a continuum of internal, vs external, control significantly influences the decisions one makes, one's personal attainment, success, and happiness. Those operating on the <u>internal control</u> end of the spectrum experience the most positive results. He found that people with a more internal sense of control:

- Are more likely to engage in activities that improve their circumstances.
- Work harder to develop knowledge, skills and abilities.
- Are more inquisitive and analytical in evaluating outcomes.
- Are more focused on achievement.

- Tend to work harder and persevere longer
- Learn more from their experiences, which they then apply to future situations.

This does not mean you can have total control. Occasionally things will happen to you over which you have no control, but you always have control of how you chose to *respond* to those factors. Whenever tempted to think that some person or something is "ruining your life", look in the mirror. It is almost always you doing the ruining. Playing the "victim" is a disastrous way to go through life.

Recognize that you always have a choice and that choosing not to choose is a choice in itself. Developing your decision making and problem-solving skills enhances your control. Don't let circumstances and other people control your life.

CHANGE

Change is not a four-letter word! We should embrace, not avoid change, provided the change is positive. Some contend that resistance to change is human nature. I believe that is a cop-out. Change sometimes involves effort. Some fear change means loss of control. Typically, effort and fear are what generate resistance to change.

Everything in life changes. Everything! Change is another word for evolution. *How* we evolve is our choice. *That* we evolve is not. Life is a process of continuous change. The world is constantly changing. If we don't change, we lose touch with reality. Learning changes (expands, alters) our minds. Change is how we grow.

> "The world as we have created it is a result of our thinking. It cannot be changed without changing our thinking."
>
> Albert Einstein

We are constantly making decisions, big and small. These choices are about who we are and what we will change and how. Each night when we go to bed we are different from the person we were when we got up. Our challenge is to make the changes positive and productive.

> "Incredible change happens in your life when you decide to take control of what you do have power over, instead of craving control over what you don't."
> Steve Maraboli

We are all involved in many roles: spouse, parent, sibling, son, daughter, student, employee, supervisor, group member, friend, etc. etc. Striving to become better at fulfilling those roles is a worthwhile objective. It enriches our lives and the lives of others. Becoming stagnant or failing to fulfil our responsibilities in these roles means falling short of our potential.

> "Progress is impossible without change and those who cannot change their minds, cannot change anything."
> George Bernard Shaw

I spent part of my career as a management consultant. Early in every consulting assignment I made a short presentation to the client and staff along these lines:

> "We are here because we want things to change.

> You have chosen to retain my company's services because you are dissatisfied with the status quo. You want things to be better. Things will not get better unless we change things.

> One definition of insanity is: 'doing the same thing over and over again and expecting different results'.

If we want better results, we have to change behavior. To change behavior, we have to change peoples' minds. Results will not improve without changes."

This is as true for individuals as it is for organizations. If you want your life to be more fulfilling, you must change mindset and behavior. Resisting change is self-limiting. It shuts off possibilities and opportunities.

The attitude that we are helpless victims of our history or our circumstances is a cop out. We all have the ability to change.

> "For what it's worth: it's never too late or, too early to be whoever you want to be. There's no time limit, stop whenever you want. You can change or stay the same, there are no rules to this thing. We can make the best or the worst of it. I hope you make the best of it. And I hope you see things that startle you. I hope you feel things you never felt before. I hope you meet people with a different point of view. I hope you live a life you're proud of. If you find that you're not, I hope you have the courage to start all over again."
> Eric Roth

Our focus should be on how to make changes that make us, our relationships and the world better, not worse. Resolving and striving to become better persons and to help improve the lives of others are worthwhile goals, and increase the probability that inevitable changes will be positive.

Change for the sake of change is a waste. Change for improvement is worthwhile. Improvement will not happen without change.

CHANGE – don't fight it, promote it!

> "Be the change that you wish to see in the world."
> Mahatma Gandhi

FAIRNESS & JUSTICE

Fairness and justice embrace the concepts of doing what is *right*, what is consistent with accepted standards of conduct and what is impartial and non-discriminatory.

These terms also have subtle, and not so subtle, nuances and interpretations that can at times conflict, and cause conflicts. "Fair" to some means equal, as in everyone should be treated equally. To others it may mean that everyone should get what they deserve, as in rewards should be related to effort. Those who produce/contribute more should get more. Those who are lazy and shiftless should get less. Still another perspective is that fairness means fulfilling one's responsibilities to those in society with the greatest needs. That those who have more have an obligation to give more to those who have less. How to do the fair and just thing is not always crystal clear. We must try anyway. Think about it.

Don't expect life to be fair or that justice will always prevail. The history of this country and the world is replete with injustice, especially for those who are "different". Some contend that the fact that 30% of Americans are people of color, yet 60% of the population of the nation's prisons are people of color, is an indication that the "system" is biased. Others would contend that the statistic is justified.

The Euro-American justice system is based upon principles of punishment and retribution. The underlying logic is that, because the offender has caused a victim to suffer, the offender should be made to suffer. It is an adversarial system designed to satisfy the victim's and society's desire for revenge.

Some Eastern cultures and the Indigenous People of this continent had/have a different approach for dealing with justice. The focus is upon the restoration of balance and harmony between the offended and the offender, and the offender and the community. The emphasis is on mending. The objective is to make amends and restore relationships. Often this is accomplished through compensation, rather than punishment.

It is in no way "fair" that some are born with physical limitations/defects, some contract debilitating diseases and others stay healthy, some of us are obese and waste food, while thousands of children die every day from starvation and malnutrition.

The fact is, life is not fair, is not just. Our systems of justice are imperfect. In spite of all that, we should personally strive to be fair and just and to do everything we can to promote fairness and justice.

WORK

How we view work has a lot to do with our comfort level with life. If we view work as punishment, drudgery, a necessary evil, the price we have to pay to make a living, chances are we will: not do it very well. We will derive little satisfaction from it and will find our lives full of stress. If we don't do it very well, it is not likely to impress those to whom we are responsible, which will inevitably lead to more stress.

> "Work done for a reward is much lower than work done in the Yoga of wisdom. Set thy heart upon the work, but never on its reward. Work not for the reward; but never cease to do thy work."
> The Bhagavad Gita

If we view work as a challenge, an opportunity to learn, grow, and demonstrate our abilities to do "good" work, it can be a source of pride, self-esteem and satisfaction. No matter the level of responsibility, even if it is sweeping streets, doing well

what we do is important; emotionally, psychologically and monetarily.

> "Today and every day deliver more than you are getting paid to do. The victory of success will be half won when you learn the secret of putting out more than is expected in all that you do. Make yourself so valuable in your work that eventually you will become indispensable. Exercise your privilege to go the extra mile, and enjoy all the rewards you receive. You deserve them."
>
> Og Mandino

We should develop a positive perspective about work. Often the best results of doing work well is not what you get for it, but what you become from it.

AGING

I'm beginning to think about getting old someday (not now, but someday), so I found George Carlin's comments about "aging" amusing:

> **"Do you realize that the only time in our lives when we like to get old is when we're kids? If you're less than 10 years old, you're so excited about aging that you think in fractions. 'How old are you?' 'I'm four and a half' You're never thirty-six and a half. You're four and a half, going on five! That's the key.**
>
> **You get into your teens, now they can't hold you back. You jump to the next number, or even a few ahead. 'How old are you?" I'm gonna be '16'. You may be 13, but hey, you're gonna be 16.**
>
> **And then the greatest day of your life! You become 21- Even the words sound like a ceremony. YOU BECOME 21. YESSSS!!!**

But then you turn 30. Oooohh, what happened there? Makes you sound like bad milk. He TURNED; we had to throw him out. There's no fun now, you're Just a sour-dumpling. What's wrong? What's changed?

You BECOME 21, you TURN 30, then you're PUSHING 40. Whoa, Put on the brakes, it's all slipping away. Before you know it, you REACH 50 and your dreams are gone...

But wait, You MAKE it to 60. You didn't think you would! So you BECOME 21, TURN 30, PUSH 40, REACH 50 and MAKE it to 60.

You've built up so much speed that you HIT 70. After that it's a day-by day thing; you HIT Wednesday.

You get into your 80's and every day is a complete cycle; you HIT lunch; you TURN 4:30; you REACH bedtime. And it doesn't end there. Into the 90s, you start going backwards; 'I Was JUST 92.'

Then a strange thing happens. If you make it over 100, you become a little kid again. 'I'm 100 and a half'.

MAY YOU ALL MAKE IT TO A HEALTHY 100 AND A HALF!

Every physical fitness, food supplement, weight loss pill, and cosmetic company has a "secret" for keeping us young. Carlin has his own version.

HOW TO STAY YOUNG

1. Throw out nonessential numbers. This includes age, weight and height. Let the doctors worry about them. That is why you pay them.

2. Keep only cheerful friends. The grouches pull you down.

3. Keep learning. Learn more about the computer, crafts, gardening, whatever, even ham radio. Never let the brain idle. 'An idle mind is the devil's workshop. 'And the devil's family name is Alzheimer's

4. Enjoy the simple things.

5. Laugh often, long and loud. Laugh until you gasp for breath.

6. The tears happen. Endure, grieve, and move on. The only person, who is with us our entire life, is ourselves. Be ALIVE while you are alive.

7. Surround yourself with what you love, whether it's family, pets, keepsakes, music, books, plants, hobbies, whatever. Your home is your refuge.

8. Cherish your health: If it is good, preserve it. If it is unstable, improve it. If it is beyond what you can improve, get help.

9. Don't take guilt trips. Take a trip to the mall, even to the next county; to a foreign country, but NOT to where the guilt is.

10. Tell the people you love that you love them, at every opportunity.

AND ALWAYS REMEMBER:

Life is not measured by the number of breaths we take, but by the moments that take our breath away. We all need to live life to its fullest each day.

The purpose of life's journey is not to arrive at the grave safely, in a well-preserved body, but rather to skid in sideways, totally worn out .... Shouting "WHAT A RIDE". Enjoy the ride. There are no return tickets."

George Carlin

PART III. HOW SHOULD I CHOOSE TO LIVE MY LIFE?

THE GOLDEN RULE

"Do unto others what you would have them do unto you."

This simple, yet immensely powerful, concept has the potential to change lives (especially our own) and the world.

Think about how different the world would be if we would all just follow this basic guideline for respecting the value of other lives. There would be no war, no crime no hatred, no class conflict, no social strife. In this simple concept, humankind has literally had for centuries the answer to most of the world's problems, but refuses to recognize and implement that answer.

Many of us acknowledge the wisdom of the message, but fail to follow it for a variety of reasons: We are focused on "me" and what's in it for "me". We are distrustful and fearful of those of different skin colors, religions, social class, language, etc.. It violates our sense of what is "fair" – "people treat me poorly, why should I be nice to them."; etc. etc. None of which are legitimate reasons for not doing what is admittedly hard work.

This is not a new concept, nor, as we Christians like to believe, is it unique to Christianity. We associate it with Jesus's Sermon on the Mount, when in fact the concept was recognized as foundational and critical to human relationships by many cultures hundreds of years before Jesus preached its value. I was interested to find the following examples:

> "In everything, do to others what you would have them do to you. Matthew: 7:12, Luke, 6:31

"You shall love your neighbor as yourself"   Matthew 22:40

"Hurt not others with that which pains yourself" – Buddhism

"Do not impose on others what you yourself do not desire" – Confucius

"This is the sum of duty: do naught to others which if done to thee would cause thee pain. - Hinduism

"No one of you is a believer until he desires for his brother that which he desires for himself. – Islam

"What is hateful to you, do not do to your neighbor." – Judaism/Talmud

"Whatever is disagreeable to yourself do not do unto others." – Zoroastrianism

"Chose thou for thy neighbor that which thou chooseth for thyself." - Baha'i

"One who is going to take a pointed stick to pinch a baby bird should first try it on himself to feel how it hurts." - Nigerian Proverb.

"A man should wander about treating all creatures as he himself would be treated." -Jainism

I particularly like the Nigerian version. Note that the Jainism version extends the courtesy to all creatures.

If we would but follow the Golden Rule we would feel good about ourselves and make the world a better place because of our contributions. The Golden Rule has "Golden Possibilities". **PRACTICE IT.** If we were each to vow every morning that today we will treat others as we would like to be treated, regardless of how they treat us, our lives would be richer and far less stressful, and the world would be a better place.

SERVICE - HOW WILL I "GIVE BACK"?

Life itself is a gift we did nothing to earn. In addition, no one makes it through life entirely on his or her own merits. We all owe others. Life is a blessing we should acknowledge by contributing to the lives of others. Living a meaningful life means making the world a better place because we lived.

> "Life's most persistent and urgent question is: What are you doing for others?"
> Dr. Martin Luther King Jr

Giving back is a win-win proposition. By serving, we not only improve the lives of others, but also reap personal benefits. A Harvard Business School study confirmed that: "happier people give more and giving makes people happier, such that happiness and giving may operate in a positive feedback loop." Those who receive help are grateful for the help and volunteers learn that helping others makes them feel better. Unlike giving money, giving time, energy and effort directly, provides immediate feedback about what your contribution means to those receiving it. Our lives are richer, more full and complete through attending to the healing of others.

> "Service to others is the rent you pay for your room here in earth."
> Muhammad Ali

Giving generates hope. We can each be part of the problem or part of the solution.

> "There is a light in the world, a healing spirit more powerful than any darkness we may encounter. We sometimes lose sight of this force when there is suffering, too much pain. Then suddenly, the spirit will emerge through the lives of ordinary people who hear a call and answer in extraordinary ways."
> Mother Teresa

Consider being one of those who hears and answers. We each have something to offer. Giving should not be driven by feelings of guilt or obligation, but by an expression of gratitude that we have the ability, and a response to the understanding that we are all interrelated and interdependent.

> "An individual has not started living until he can rise above the narrow confines of his individualistic concerns to the broader concerns of all humanity."
> Martin Luther King, Jr.

A defining factor in living a meaningful life is contributing to something above and beyond self.

> "The best way to find yourself is to lose yourself in the service of others."
> Mahatma Ghandi

We should consciously choose to invest time where our efforts will yield a return for others. Gifts do not have to be costly. The gift of friendship or simply one's presence can make a difference in someone's life.

> "The founding of temples is meritorious, meditations and religious exercises pacify the heart, comprehension of the truth leads to Nirvana – but greater than all is loving-kindness. As the light of the moon is sixteen

times greater than the light of all the stars, so is loving-kindness sixteen times more efficacious in liberating the heart than all other religious accomplishments taken together. This state of the heart is the best in the world."
The Buddha

When selecting an area in which to give back, it is important to select a cause in which one has an interest and abilities. That makes it more fun. Do something. Make a commitment. It is better if it represents an on-going commitment rather than a one-time shot. Finding a way to help people help themselves can be particularly rewarding.

"When you learn, teach. When you get, give."
Maya Angelou

The following is a list of several ways one can give back. It is by no means exhaustive. Think of some others you can add in the spaces. For more ideas, take a look at this website -- *www.volunteermatch.org*.

OPPORTUNITIES TO GIVE BACK

1. Visit someone in a nursing home.
2. Volunteer at your local animal shelter.
3. Organize a Park Cleanup with friends.
4. Help with yard work for elderly or unwell neighbors.
5. Volunteer at a local soup kitchen.
6. Become a mentor to a young person.
7. Volunteer at an After School program.
8. Donate your hair to charities like Wigs for Kids or Children With Hair Loss.
9. Donate blood at the Red Cross.
10. Collect and donate gently used coats and sweatshirts to a local charity.
11. Teach English as a second language as a literacy volunteer.

12. Tutor students.
13. Volunteer to help build homes with Habitat for Humanity.
14. Register to become an organ donor.
15. Volunteer at an equine therapy center.
16. Coach a local youth team.
17. Volunteer at Meals on Wheels.
18. Volunteer at a Hospital.
19. Recycle.
20. Volunteer at a Wilderness Center.
21. Volunteer to read to kids at the local library, nursery or preschool.
22. Collect food to donate to food pantries.
23. Volunteer at a local non-profit agency. Check with the United Way for suggestions and contacts.
24. Organize a fund-raising event for a local charity.
25. Volunteer with an Adaptive Sports Program.
26. _____
27. _____
28. _____
29. _____
30. _____

In the final analysis, all we really own is our lives. It is how we use our lives that determines what kind of people we are. It is by serving and giving that we find life.

RELATIONSHIPS & FRIENDSHIPS

> "There is no enjoying the possession of anything valuable unless one has someone to share it with."
> Seneca

In discussing a Harvard Medical School decades long study of factors that contribute to a life considered well lived, Dr. George Vaillant, who followed the results of the study for over

20 years, was quoted as saying: "the only thing that really matters in life are your relationships to other people."

The study confirmed that, when assessing the "success" of their lives, the participants rated connectedness to family, friends, neighbors and co-workers, as the most important contributor.

Relationships matter! They enrich our lives. How then should we treat them?

Cherish Family - Ties to family are extremely important. From family a child forms values, develops a sense of safety and belonging, develops aspirations, learns to love and to manage human relationships. What a child learns in family forms communities, societies, nations and the world.

Children learn from instruction, but they learn more indelibly from example. They model what they see demonstrated by parents, siblings and others of influence. As adults, we typically underestimate this effect. Children will do what we do, much more readily than what we say. This places on parents, older siblings and adults a huge responsibility to be appropriate role models.

We should: value family, make family a priority, always be there for family, provide support when needed, be loyal to family, enjoy family, create and nurture family traditions and strengthen and nurture family relationships.

> "What do most people say on their deathbeds? They don't say 'I wish I had made more money'. What they say is: 'I wish I had spent more time with my family'".
> David Rubenstein

One of the things I respect most about my Amish friends is their commitment to family. They don't send kids to orphanages or their old folks to nursing homes, to be cared for by strangers. They take care of their young and their old. Family is important. Family assumes responsibility for family.

> "The only things that are really permanent are love, family and friendship. At the end of the day, that's what it really boils down to. The rest is just stuff."

Jared Kushner

We Are All Related - Relationships with those outside the immediate family are important as well. There is an increasing awareness in some circles that we are all related, and that this has significant implications. The Indigenous People of this country seemed to grasp this concept.

One of the more unique aspects of traditional Native American culture is the depth of understanding and appreciation of the interconnectedness and interdependence of all people and all things. This concept was often expressed with the phrase: *"we are all related"*. In the Sioux cultures, prayers are often concluded with the phrase "for all my relations". All my relations includes: family, tribe, all the nations of two leggeds in the world, the four leggeds, the winged creatures and all the earth's living things.

Native Americans were not the first to understand this truth. In the 6th century BCE, the Buddha said:

> "The practice of making others happy is based upon the clear understanding of life which is Oneness. In deep gratitude, let us realize this Oneness of all life, the heart of which is compassion."

In the first century, a Stoic philosopher wrote:

> "All that you behold, that which comprises both god and man, is one – we are the parts of one great body."
> Seneca

This concept, that everything within the universe is living and related, has moral implications. It means we each have a responsibility to care for all living things, to maintain balance and harmony in the world, and to demonstrate respect for all things that live. Because we are all related, we should strive to live in harmony with all people and all living things.

In the book *GROUNDED*, published in 2015, Diana Butler Bass explains the 'Big Bang' theory of creation in this way:

> "The big bang's simplest insight, and the one with the most profound implications for understanding God and contemporary spirituality, is straightforward: everything that exists was created at the same time; thus all things are connected by virtue of being made of the same matter. This dust (matter) has, throughout time, formed and reformed into gases, worlds and living beings......According to this scientific theory, everything is connected with everything else. Quite literally, Human Beings, (and everything else) are made of stardust."

In her book *THE SACRED DEPTHS OF NATURE,* Ursula Goodenough, one of America's premier biologists, states the following:

> "So, all the creatures on the planet today share a huge number of genetic ideas. Most of my genes are like most gorilla genes, but they're also like many of the genes in a mushroom. I have more genes than a mushroom, to be sure, and some critical genes are certainly different, but the important piece to take in here is our deep interrelatedness, our deep genetic homology, with the rest of the living world."
> Goodenough p 72.

Scientists are not the only group of moderns who have embraced this concept of interrelatedness. In a book titled *PROCESS THEOLOGY,* Bruce G. Epperly lists the following among what he labels the "Essential Concepts of Process Theology":

- "All living things exist in relationship with one another. We live in an interdependent universe in which each moment of experience arises from its environment, whose influence provides both limits and possibilities."
- "Experience is universal, though variable, and extends beyond humankind. While creatures differ in complexity and impact on the world, every creature has some minimal level of responsiveness to its environment."
- "The universality of experience leads to the recognition that every creature is inherently valuable and deserves moral consideration.
- Process Theology values all creation, even apart from its impact on human life… flora and fauna are valuable not just because we appreciate their beauty but because they experience some level of joy and sorrow. They matter to God and, accordingly, should enter into our own moral calculations."

In his book; *A SEEKER'S THEOLOGY,* John Macort, a retired Episcopal Priest who taught in Catholic schools and later became a practicing Quaker, wrote:

"We are all related as we share that divine Existence with God. We are all united as One."

In his book, *ETERNAL LIFE: A NEW VISION,* John Shelby Spong wrote:

"In fact we now know that all matter within our universe, from the farthest star to the content of your body and mine is interconnected. Such a sense of interdependency has, before our time, never even been imagined. Human life is kin not just to the great apes but to the cabbages and indeed even to the plankton in the sea... That insight leads to the conclusion that while separation may have been our perception, it is not the law of the universe. A deep interrelated unity is."

Despite their differences in perspective, scientists and theologians are reaching the same conclusions as did the Indigenous People of this continent - every living thing is interconnected and interdependent - We Are All Related.

Our world would be an immeasurably better place — a place of balance, harmony and peace — if we could learn to treat all humans as brothers and sisters and all living things as sacred, and thus worthy of respect.

There are certain **principles** that have proven effective for making relationships work:

Earn Trust - Trust is the foundation of all effective relationships. In *The Speed of Trust*, Stephen M. R. Covey wrote:

> "There is one thing that is common to every individual, relationship, team, family, organization, nation, economy, and civilization throughout the world - one thing which, if removed, will destroy the most powerful government,; the most successful business, the most thriving economy, the most influential leadership, the greatest friendship, the strongest character, the deepest love. On the other hand, if developed and leveraged, that one thing has the potential to create unparalleled success and prosperity in every dimension of life. Yet,

it is the least understood, most neglected, and most underestimated possibility of our time. That one thing is trust."

Trust is built on integrity and competence. It must be earned. We earn trust by meeting commitments, telling the truth, and doing what we say we are going to do. Being trustworthy means those with whom we interact are confident of our motives, our ethics, our reliability and our abilities.

Trust is crucial. EARN IT!

Be Real – To develop meaningful relationships requires that we be real, that we drop pretenses and reveal our true feelings and our true selves. Being authentic means admitting you are a work in progress and are not perfect. It means being genuinely empathetic.

We should forget about trying to be impressive and instead strive to be real.

A key lesson in life is to understand our real selves, to be real in our relationships and to see the authenticity in others.

Demonstrate Respect - Effective people have well established standards and expectations for personal relationships. Principles for relationships are based upon assumptions of mutual respect. Some of the principles considered necessary for achieving harmonious relationships are as follow:

- Always tell the truth. Lying destroys relationships
- Listen carefully.
- Never interrupt when another is talking.
- Seek to understand. Visualize yourself in the other person's "shoes".
- Be honest.
- Keep commitments.
- Accept responsibility for your words and actions.

Think Win/Win - Many significant decisions involve interactions with others. Covey, in *The Seven Habits*, contends that to make these decisions effective, they should be constructed as "Win/Win".

> "Win/Win is a frame of mind and heart that constantly seeks mutual benefit in human interactions. Win/Win means that agreements or solutions are mutually beneficial, mutually satisfying. With Win/Win solutions, all parties feel good about the decision and feel committed to the action plan."

Covey continues:

> "Win/Win is based on the paradigm that there is plenty for everybody, that one person's success is not achieved at the expense or exclusion of the success of others. Win/Win is a belief in the Third Alternative. It's not your way or my way; it's a better way, a higher way."

Each of us is the common denominator in all of our relationships. The attitude that we bring to the relationship determines the quality thereof. Every relationship, no matter how brief, is potentially important because it may alter someone's life. Strive to make all your relationships WIN/WIN, for all involved.

INCLUSIVE vs EXCLUSIVE

Some of our most important decisions involve how we view and relate to other people. One of the greatest sources of strife, conflict, suffering and inhumanity in the world, today and historically, is humankind's attitude toward, and reaction to differences in: race, religion and culture. Unconscionable atrocities have been committed against fellow humans because they looked, thought, believed and/or prayed differently than the perpetrators. These atrocities were the result of personal and collective decisions.

> "I happen to think that the singular evil of our time is prejudice. It is from this evil that all other evils grow and multiply."
>
> Rod Sterling

People all too often react to personal differences with fear, mistrust and misunderstanding. What we desperately need is an awareness and appreciation of, and a commitment to, genuine, inclusive community, with the term community encompassing family, neighborhood, country, and world. We are all in this together, whether we realize it or not. No matter how much we value our independence, we are mutually dependent.

> "You're not under attack when others gain rights and privileges you've always had."
>
> DaShanne Stokes

> "The way to be successful is to find a way to be inclusive of everybody. It's the difference between an attitude that looks at diversity and assumes you can be successful despite it, versus an attitude that looks at diversity and assumes you can be successful as a result of it."
>
> "Magic" Johnson

Tolerance or Acceptance - Intolerance is despicable, but tolerance is insufficient. We need to do more than tolerate those unlike us. The difference between tolerance and acceptance is huge. "I tolerate" means I consider myself superior to, but I will allow the existence of others, as long as they do not impinge on my own life and way of doing things, or encroach on my value systems. To simply tolerate means to barely notice that others exist and to have as little as possible to do with them.

> "The world is getting too small for both an Us and a Them. Us and Them have become codependent, intertwined, fixed to one another. We have no separate fates, but are bound together in one. And our fear of one another is the only thing capable of our undoing."
> Sam Killermann

To accept others means placing ourselves on the same level, genuinely getting to know the other, allowing the other the same rights we expect, and attempting to understand each other, despite any differences. It means respecting another's right to be different and attempting to learn by really listening to the perspectives of others.

> "Beware of the differences that blind us to the unity that binds us."
> Huston Smith

When we speak of inclusiveness, we are not talking about uniformity, but about a mindset that values and celebrates differences. Humans desperately need community. A group based on exclusivity is not a community, but a clique. Real communities are inclusive.

> "Inclusion works to the advantage of everyone. We all have things to learn and we all have something to teach."
> Helen Henderson

"Loving your neighbor as yourself" is a quotation usually associated with Christianity, but the closely related "do unto others as you would have them do unto you" is a basic value common to many cultures. Living these values is a personal responsibility and should be incorporated into all personal and group relationships.

I noticed the following on a poster in a church window. I thought it so relevant that I parked the car and went back and copied it down:

LOVE YOUR NEIGHBOR WHO DOESN'T
LOOK LIKE YOU
THINK LIKE YOU
LOVE LIKE YOU
SPEAK LIKE YOU
PRAY LIKE YOU
VOTE LIKE YOU
LOVE YOUR NEIGHBOR,
NO EXCEPTIONS

Values and principles are learned, primarily from family and friends. Children are not born with exclusivity, intolerance and bigotry built in. They have to be taught. In the early 1950's, Rogers and Hammerstein expressed this truth through the words of a song in the score of the musical *SOUTH PACIFIC*:

> "they have to be taught before it's too late before they are six or seven or eight to hate all the people their relatives hate they have to be carefully taught."

We must carefully teach our children inclusiveness, acceptance and respect for human dignity. As with most values, we most effectively teach these by example.

Being an inclusive person means:

- Communicating honestly with each other
- Respecting and celebrating human differences
- Transcending differences rather than attempting to obliterate them

- Genuinely demonstrating an interest in the values, beliefs and worldviews of others
- Showing empathy – the willingness to share the burdens of others.
- Building relationships that go deeper than superficial niceties
- Committing to: understand each other, rejoice together, mourn together and find delight in each other.

Seek out and learn from those who are "different". Make a personal decision to embrace inclusiveness.

> "We need to give each other space so that we may both give and receive such beautiful things as ideas, openness, dignity, joy, healing, and inclusion."
> Max de Pree

Compassion - Demonstrating compassion, the sharing of someone's pain, discomfort, dilemma, loss or unfortunate circumstance, is almost always the "right" thing to do. It is helpful to care enough to take on some of the burden, so that another person does not have to bear problems alone.

Generosity - Generosity is rooted in the belief that we receive many gifts and thus have the obligation and privilege to "give back". Giving to another enhances the development of relationships, and reinforces the perception that a "good" person is one who shares.

Gratitude - We sometimes are so obsessed with what we want that we fail to appreciate what we have. We are all blessed in multiple ways and have much for which we should be grateful.

> "When you arise in the morning, think of what a precious privilege it is to be alive, to breathe, to think, to enjoy, to love."
> Marcus Aurelius

Feeling and expressing appreciation for those blessings is a basic obligation. An appropriate principle is to expect nothing and appreciate the value of everything.

> "Gratitude unlocks the fullness of life. It turns what we have into enough, and more."
> Melody Beattie

Gratitude is more than an obligation. Studies show that it has personal benefits for the one demonstrating it. Sonja Lyubomirsky, in her book *The How of Happiness*, writes:

> "People who are consistently grateful have been found to be relatively happier, more energetic, and more hopeful, and to report experiencing more frequent positive emotions. They also tend to be more helpful and empathic, more spiritual and religious, more forgiving, and less materialistic than others who are less predisposed to gratefulness. Furthermore, the more a person is inclined to gratitude, the less likely he or she is to be depressed, anxious, lonely, envious or neurotic."

Feeling and expressing gratitude is not only the right thing to do, it has positive personal rewards.

Friendship - Friendship is a very special kind of relationship. We all need friends. Numerous studies show that there is a direct relationship between happiness and the breadth and depth of one's friendships. A friend is someone who can sense what a friend needs and is ever willing to help meet that need. Making friends and keeping friends is not always easy. The way to have the kinds of friends we want and need, is to be the kind of friend we want to have.

- Be a good listener and don't try to dominate conversations. People often need to "unload", to air their concerns and problems. Having someone they can trust to share their burdens is a real asset.
- Never attempt to persuade a friend to do something that is inconsistent with her/his values or ethics.
- Take the initiative. Demonstrate that you wish to be friendly. People often confuse reticence with arrogance.
- Demonstrate real interest in the friend's life and what interests him/her.
- Be slow to judge. Be willing to get to know a person's true character.
- Be willing to forgive small mistakes. Don't expect friends to be perfect, but set limits.
- Be loyal to friends. Don't criticize them behind their backs or break confidences. Defend them without being untruthful.
- Act like you want your friends to act.
- Keep promises.
- Perform small acts of kindness.
- When you make a mistake, say "I'm sorry".
- Compassionately help friends with shortcomings, but don't become a critic. Criticism does not build friendships.
- Encourage friends to be their best and support their positive efforts.

When choosing friends, (it is your choice), consider the above as criteria. Choose wisely because one tends to become like those with whom one associates. While true friends are important, don't become friend dependent. Friends are human and imperfect. Don't let them control who you are. Choose friends based on character, not wealth, social status or

58

popularity. The test of true friendship is whether or not you are a better person when you are with that friend. Choose well.

When you have a true friend, let the friend know how important you consider the friendship to be.

Parenting - If you have been blessed with children, you have taken on the most important job in the world, and the <u>most difficult</u>.

It is tough to teach kids about integrity, morality, ethical behavior, responsibility, compassion, relationships, self-control and service when the world in which they function is awash with drug abuse, assault, alcoholism, rape, suicides, in-school shootings, unplanned pregnancies, and robbery, but it has to be done.

Young people need to understand that all their actions have consequences, that drugs and alcohol kill people regularly, that you are always there for them, that your love is unconditional, but your approval is not.

Understand that example is the most powerful teacher. Young people are much more likely to do what you do than to do what you say.

Help your children understand that they are loved, valuable, unique, and a storehouse of potential.

Give your children your attention. In his book, *How Then Shall We Live,* Wayne Muller reminds us of this truth about parental love:

> "Attention is the manifestation of love. If I keep pushing my children away when they want me to play with them, they do not feel loved. I may have love in my heart; I may feel joy when I see them, and want only the best for them. But they will feel my love only

when I turn around and give them my undivided attention. Through my attention, they experience my love."

BEAUTY

There is beauty all around us, but we often miss it. We are naturally drawn to beauty, but get distracted by "entertainment" and mental clutter. Beauty can be seen, heard, sensed or felt. Beauty is something that generates in us a feeling of pleasure. Roses, sunsets, mountains, good music, the face of a sleeping baby, are all beautiful, but so also are acts of compassion and kindness. Beauty is physical, emotional and spiritual.

"Begin with the beautiful, and it leads you to the true."
Father Robert Barron

Beauty satisfies us, comforts us, inspires us, adds meaning to our lives. Recognizing and adding to the beauty in the world is both an obligation and a blessing.

"Let the beauty that we love be what we do."
Rumi

Walk alone and listen to the beautiful messages of the birds, the flowers, the trees, the clouds, your own mind. Be sensitive to the beauty that lies in acts of love. Don't let the beauty of the world and life escape you.

Beauty:

Look for it.
Appreciate it.
Enhance it.
Restore it.
Create it.
Live it.

BALANCE & HARMONY

We should strive to live in harmony with people and with nature. The concept includes principles for guiding one's thoughts, speech, actions and behavior. These principles represent a worldview and a philosophy, a comprehensive and complex network of ideas, encompassing both a way of living and a state of being.

The concept recognizes that individuals have the ability to choose: to positively control their lives through responsible thought, speech and behavior, or to destroy their lives and negatively impact the lives of others by thinking, speaking and behaving irresponsibly. It emphasizes accepting personal responsibility for one's actions and regularly taking corrective measures to maintain, and/or return to, balance and harmony. Looking for the beauty and lessons in every human experience helps one maintain inner harmony. The philosophy identifies key elements of moral and ethical behavior and important relationship principles necessary for living a long, harmonious and meaningful life.

The concept of balance and harmony has deep and comprehensive meaning, with these conceptually distinct characteristics:

- *Spirituality* represents the expectation that one must respect and honor the Creator through prayer, spiritual/religious practice and concern for fellow humans.
- *Respect* is the act of maintaining loyal reverence by offering respect to self, others, nature, Spirit, animals and the environment.
- *Reciprocity* represents the constant graceful and respectful exchange and receipt of support, acts of kindness, helpfulness, and tokens of appreciation or

honor. Nothing is ever received without giving back, and the virtue of generosity is essential for authentic reciprocity.

- *Discipline* represents the commitment to achieving life goals through sustaining controlled, productive daily activity in the form of study, self-care, physical activity, and helpfulness to others.
- *Thinking* represents the cognitive functioning required to maintain a consistent, positive outlook, while planning and organizing the present and future.
- *Relationships* – are to be honored, recognizing our connectedness to Spirit, family, community, all the peoples of the world, nature and the universe. A constant awareness of the interdependence between oneself and others is required.

The concept of balance and harmony encompasses the meanings of the words: beauty, goodness, well-being, happiness, completeness, perfection and order. It means living the "right way". It means seeking harmony and balance within one's self, with other persons, with all living things and with one's natural environment. It includes seeking and respecting the beauty in all things.

Harmony and interconnectedness are closely related concepts.

> "Everything is connected. The wing of the corn beetle affects the direction of the wind, the way the sand drifts, the way the light reflects into the eye of man beholding his reality. All is part of totality, and in this totality, man finds his hozho, his way of walking in harmony, with beauty all around him."
>
> Tony Hillerman - Author

Living in right relationships requires that one be aware and receptive, recognizing that everything that happens to us has a message for us, something for us to learn. We should listen for, and be receptive to, these messages. Reflecting on both positive and negative experiences, we should ask ourselves:

- "What is this experience teaching me about myself, about others and about living?"
- "What am I teaching others through the way that I live?"

Michael Garrett, *WRITTEN ON THE WIND*

Choosing Balance and Harmony - Finding balance and harmony depends upon making the right choices. Making the right choices often depends on asking the right questions. Seeking and understanding basic truths helps one make the right choices.

Finding balance and harmony in our lives is not easy. Life is full of struggles to find the correct balance between conflicting demands, aspirations and priorities. Finding and adhering to the "right" balance between family and work, work and play, self-interest and the welfare of others, things material and things spiritual all involve important decisions. Living a life of balance and harmony does not mean that life will not pose difficulties and challenges. It means making choices with the intention of creating "good'.

> "Well-being occurs when we seek and find our unique place in the universe and experience the continuous cycle of receiving and giving through respect and reverence for the beauty of all living things. Stated another way, everyone and everything was created with a specific purpose to fulfill, and no one should have the

power to interfere or impose on others the best path to follow."

Michael Garrett, *WALKING ON THE WIND*,

Finding the right balance and harmony takes conscious effort. We need first to achieve internal harmony. The mind, the heart and the body must be in harmony. Harmony can best be approached by carefully selecting a set of values and principles, living a life consistent with those values and principles, being thankful, giving back and by listening to the guidance and wisdom of one's inner voice. We realize our lives are in balance and we find peace of mind and satisfaction when our values, principles, goals, attention and behavior are all in alignment.

REVERENCE FOR NATURE

Environmental quality and the quality of human life are mutually dependent. Preserving nature from the destruction of human endeavors is our moral obligation to this and future generations. We have no right to destroy the planet our grandchildren and their grandchildren will inherit. We are meant to be stewards, not exploiters, of the beauty of creation and its life giving and life enhancing functions.

The challenges of responsibly utilizing Nature's abundance are daunting, but what is inexcusable is the rampant and wanton abuse of nature for no reason at all, other than human indifference, laziness and sloth. Indifference, the mindset that "it doesn't matter", is the greatest threat to the richness and beauty of our earth, and to our future.

Choices about the goods we purchase, about production methods, about lifestyle and life practices should be consistent with the principles of "sustainability". Sustainable products and practices are those that are environmentally friendly, from extraction and creation, through disposal or termination. The entire life chain must be free of damage to the environment.

> "Man must be made conscious of his origin as a child of Nature. Brought into a right relationship with the wilderness, he would see that he was not a separate entity endowed with a divine right to subdue his fellow creatures and destroy our common heritage, but rather an integral part of a harmonious whole. He would see that his appropriation of earth's resources beyond his personal needs can only bring imbalance and beget ultimate loss and poverty for all."
>
> Linnie Marsh Wolfe

It is critical that we understand that our relationship with Nature, and the relationship of the elements of nature to each other, all are interdependent. Animals feed on plants and in turn animals are food for people. Humankind exhales carbon dioxide and inhales oxygen. Trees exhale oxygen and inhale carbon dioxide. We are part of a system of reciprocity. When we take something from Nature we should give something back, to maintain the crucial balance. We have a real and necessary responsibility for the guardianship of nature. The earth is not just a repository of natural resources to be exploited, it is a manifestation of life.

> "The Nature vision, the gift of seeing truly, with wonder and delight into the natural world, is informed by a certain attitude of reverence and respect. It is a matter of extrasensory as well as sensory perception. In addition to the eye, it involves the intelligence, the instinct and the imagination. It is the perception not only of objects and forms but also of essences and ideals."
>
> N. Scott Momaday – Kiowa

Modern environmental problems have become so serious that they constitute a global crisis. We are fouling our nest. Native Americans lived comfortably with nature for thousands of years. Conservation was a basic value of their culture. White cultures strive to <u>control</u> nature. Indigenous People focused on <u>cooperating</u> with nature.

Nature should be honored as the source of the plants, animals and water that sustain our lives. More than that, we must see ourselves as part of nature, not as some higher species empowered with the privilege of exploiting nature. We should see ourselves not as having "dominion" over nature, but as a part of nature, with respect and stewardship for all other parts. We must realize that humans are not above nature, but that humans require nature to make humans "whole".

Any desecration of nature, or taking from nature more than one requires, should be viewed as stealing from one's children and grandchildren and all future generations.

> "Treat the earth well: it was not given to you by your parents, it was loaned to you   by your children. We do not inherit the Earth from our ancestors, we borrow it from our children."
> Ancient Native American Proverb

> "Every human being has a sacred duty to protect the welfare of Mother Earth,   from whom all life comes. In order to do this, we must recognize the enemy...the one within us. We must begin with ourselves."
> Leon Shenandoah – Onadaga Chief

Human-kind's responsibilities to Nature include:

- Continually giving thanks for the life giving power of the sun, for the earth and the water and food the earth provides.

- Never taking more than one needs.
- Giving thanks for what we do take.
- Replenishing what is taken.
- Doing as little damage as possible.
- Taking time to appreciate the beauty of the earth.

> "The lands of the planet call to human-kind for redemption. But it is a redemption of sanity, not a supernatural reclamation project at the end of history. The planet itself calls to the other living species for relief. Religion cannot be kept within the bounds of sermons and scriptures. It is a force in and of itself and calls for the integration of lands and peoples in harmonious unity. The land waits for those who can discern its rhythms ... and for relief from the constant burden of exploitation."
>
> Vine Deloria Jr. *GOD IS RED*

Too many people just don't "get it".

> "When you have pollution in one place, it spreads all over, just as arthritis or cancer spreads in the body. The earth is sick now because the earth is being mistreated. It is very important for people to understand this. The earth is a living organism which has a will and wants to be well. Too many people don't know that when they harm the earth they harm themselves and when they harm themselves, they harm the earth."
>
> Rolling Thunder - Cherokee

In *VOICES IN THE STONES*, Kent Nerburn quotes a Native American elder who said:

> "Nature has rules. Nature has laws. You think that you can ignore the rules or, if you don't like them, you can

change them. But Mother Earth doesn't change the rules. When you can count the animals, you're getting near the end of your chances. We can count the eagles. We can count the buffalo. I've heard that in India and Africa they can count the tigers and the elephants. That's Mother Earth crying out. She's giving us a warning and She's begging for her life. And here's what your people don't ever seem to learn. There's going to become a day when things can't be fixed. And you know what? It's going to be a day just like today."

Nature as Teacher - Nature is a vast reservoir of knowledge to be tapped by observation and experience. Humans are not distinct from nature, but a part of nature. Every animal, every plant, every natural event has a lesson to convey. Observe how animals and birds care for their families. Observe what a tree limb's reaction to the wind has to teach us about the need for flexibility in our lives. By understanding nature, we can better understand ourselves. Humankind's role is to discover the rules of the universe and to learn to live in a right relationship with them. Everything that happens has a message, something to be learned. To learn from nature involves the use of all our senses. It requires that we become involved with nature and that we become constantly observant and aware. Nature has much to teach us, if we will but open our minds.

> "It remains for us to learn once again that we are a part of nature, not a transcendent species with no responsibilities to the natural world."
>
> Vine Deloria Jr., *GOD IS RED*

Indigenous People found meaning in their relationship to, and love for, Mother Earth and her creatures. If we care, observe and listen, we can do likewise.

EXPERIENCES

Seek out and learn from experiences. Experiences open our eyes to truth and understanding. Education is not just about learning facts. Education is about participating in life and learning as one participates. Involvement is key to understanding. Observe, listen and reflect. Every choice, every action has consequences. Examine them to unlock the lessons to be learned.

Make a list of the seven to ten most significant experiences of your life to date. Then note what lessons you learned from each. Consider both positive and negative lessons. Think about how you can apply those lessons to future decisions and circumstances.

Think about an interest you have that could be explored by a future experience. Plan it. Do it.

VOCATION

Choose a vocation carefully. One of the most critical life decisions we make is the choice of the kind of work we do. Work helps define who we are, because that is where we spend a lot of our time. Most of us spend a third or more of our waking hours at some type of occupation, and many spend far more time thinking or worrying about that activity. The wrong choice can lead to what Thoreau described as a life of "quiet desperation". In some cases the desperation can become more than "quiet".

Choose a vocation, not a job. The word vocation comes from the Latin word for "calling". Our lives will be more pleasant if we can work at something we feel "called" to do. Consciously search for a vocation that interests you, appeals to you, and one from which you can derive satisfaction, not just a living. Research jobs to learn what is actually involved.

First, know yourself. Understand your abilities, interests, and what you don't like. There are multiple "tests" available that attempt to match personal interests and abilities to vocations. Try them.

When considering what you want to do for the remainder of your working life, the following process may prove useful:

- List your strengths and weaknesses
- List your likes and don't likes
- List your vocational goals and ambitions.
- Select the income level you would like to achieve at various points in your career.
- Make a list of the occupations the fit with your self-assessment.
- Gather information about those occupations
- Narrow your list to the few that most interest you.
- Conduct further research. Talk to people in those occupations. Identify the educational and other requirements. Create opportunities to actually try the work to see if it fits.
- Check the alternatives against your values, goals and objectives.
- Make a choice.
- Develop a plan to make your choice happen.

Look for an opportunity to work hard at something worth doing and something you enjoy doing. The benefit of the right vocation is not how much it pays, but what you become.

Make sure that your choice is yours, not what someone thinks you should do or what is available or convenient. If your choice does not work out, don't be afraid to change. Repeat the process and try something else.

PART IV. WHAT MIGHT I DO TO IMPROVE THE QUALITY OF MY LIFE?

Many are dissatisfied with their circumstances. They either give up and blame the circumstances or make an attempt to change the circumstances. Circumstances do not make us who we are, they reveal to us who we are. We cannot always choose our circumstances, but we can always choose how we respond to circumstances, and thus control their effects.

The key to improving one's circumstances is to improve one's self. Few of us function anywhere near our capabilities. If we were to function at or near our potential, we would have few problems left to solve. We can accomplish much more than we currently envision, if we strengthen our characters and control our thoughts and actions. The following are some suggestions for taking control and improving one's lot in life.

THINK POSITIVELY

I received the following as an email from an associate. It illustrates the importance of choosing one's attitude and response to life. I thought it worth sharing.

> **"John is the kind of guy you love to hate. He is always in a good mood and always has something positive to say. When someone would ask him how he was doing, he would reply, 'If I were any better, I would be twins!"**
>
> **He was a natural motivator.**
>
> **If an employee was having a bad day, John was there telling the employee how to look on the positive side of the situation.**
>
> **Seeing this style really made me curious, so one day I went up and asked him, 'I don't get it!' 'You**

can't be a positive person all of the time. How do you do it?'

He replied, 'Each morning I wake up and say to myself, you have two choices today. You can choose to be in a good mood or...you can choose to be in a bad mood. I choose to be in a good mood.

Each time something bad happens, I can choose to be a victim or...I can choose to learn from it. I choose to learn from it.

Every time someone comes to me complaining, I can choose to accept their complaining or....I can point out the positive side of life. I choose the positive side of life.

'Yeah, right, it's not that easy,' I protested.

'Yes, it is,' he said. 'Life is all about choices. When you cut away all the junk, every situation is a choice. You choose how you react to situations. You choose how people affect your mood.

You choose to be in a good mood or bad mood. The bottom line: It's your choice how you live your life.

I reflected on what he said. Soon thereafter, I left the Tower Industry to start my own business. We lost touch, but I often thought about him when I made a choice about life, instead of reacting to it.

Several years later, I heard that he was involved in a serious accident, falling some 60 feet from a communications tower.

After 18 hours of surgery and weeks of intensive care, he was released from the hospital with rods placed in his back.

I saw him about six months after the accident.

When I asked him how he was, he replied, 'If I were any better, I'd be twins...wanna see my scars?'

I declined to see his wounds, but I did ask him what had gone through his mind as the accident took place.

'The first thing that went through my mind was the well-being of my soon-to-be born daughter,' he replied. 'Then, as I lay on the ground, I remembered that I had two choices: I could choose to live or...I could choose to die. I chose to live.'

'Weren't you scared? Did you lose consciousness?' I asked.

He continued, '....the paramedics were great. They kept telling me I was going to be fine. But when they wheeled me into the ER and I saw the expressions on the faces of the doctors and nurses, I got really scared. In their eyes, I read 'he's a dead man'. I knew I needed to take action.'

'What did you do?' I asked.

'Well, there was a big burly nurse shouting questions at me,' said John. 'She asked if I was allergic to anything 'Yes, I replied..' The doctors and nurses stopped working as they waited for my reply.. I took a deep breath and yelled, 'Gravity'.

Over their laughter, I told them, 'I am choosing to live. Operate on me as if I am alive, not dead.'

He lived, thanks to the skill of his doctors, but also because of his amazing attitude ... I learned from him that every day we have the choice to live fully.

Attitude, after all, is everything."

Life is not a problem to be solved, a burden to be endured. It is a blessing, a gift to be savored. How we view it and deal with it depends on our perspectives.

> "We often ask 'What's Wrong?' Doing so, we invite painful seeds of sorrow to come up and manifest. We feel suffering, anguish and depression, and produce much more seeds. We would be much happier if we tried to stay in touch with the healthy, joyful seeds inside of us and around us. We should learn to ask, 'What is not wrong?' and be in touch with that. There are so many elements in the world and within our bodies, feelings, perceptions, and consciousness that are wholesome, refreshing and healing. If a few block ourselves, if we stay in a prison of sorrow, we will not be in touch with these healing elements."
>
> Thich Nhat Hanh

Maintaining a positive attitude means disdaining the practices of complaining, whining and making excuses. Instead, we should focus on our blessings, be genuinely thankful and make something good happen.

WILLPOWER

A positive attitude is important, but it is not enough. If we really want to improve our lives we must take action. That takes self-discipline, willpower, self-control. We tend to attempt to avoid problems and emotional pain. Avoidance doesn't cut it. We should instead view pain and problems as challenges and understand that, although it may not be easy, we have the ability to deal with them.

Extensive research indicates that increasing willpower is the most effective tool for improving one's life. People who have better control of their actions and emotions are healthier and happier, are better able to deal with conflicts and problems, have more satisfying relationships and less stress.

Practice demonstrating willpower on small things, - eating sweets, keeping the check book balanced, – the practice improves the ability to deal effectively with more significant issues. Examine your weaknesses and plan how to avoid putting yourself in positions where your willpower might weaken. If you crave smoking, but want to stop, stay away from people who smoke. Decide in advance what you will or will not do, instead of on the spur of the moment. Meditation, focusing on breathing when your mind wanders, builds self-control. Think through and commit to simple, non-ambiguous rules for self-conduct. Make negative practices that you want to avoid, as inconvenient as possible. One study indicated that the personnel in an office cut their consumption of candy by 40% when they placed the containers in drawers rather than on desk tops.

Think positively about self-discipline. Think of it not as giving things up, but as gaining control, not as denying yourself, but as achieving something of value.

AQUIRE KNOWLEDGE, SEEK TRUTH & WISDOM

Knowledge is important and useful. Knowledge involves the awareness and understanding of facts, information and skills (knowing how to accomplish certain tasks). Knowledge is typically acquired through education and experience. Plato defined knowledge as "justified true belief". We should gain all the knowledge we can.

> "Knowledge does not mean mastering a great quantity of different information, but understanding the nature of the mind. This knowledge can penetrate each one of our thoughts and illuminate each one of our perceptions."
> Matthieu Ricard

Truth is the bedrock of morality, the highest of virtues and a powerful tool. But, truth can be illusive in this age of fake news, hype and exaggeration. We most often use the word "truth" to describe something that conforms to reality, something that is authentic or factual. It is also used to refer to the opposite of falsehood, as in telling the truth instead of lies. The search for truth is an attempt to determine the way "things really are". We should base our assessment of truth on evidence and reason. The truth can never be totally possessed, only pursued. But that in no way diminishes the value of the search. The pursuit is a worthy and rewarding one. Truth matters.

Knowledge is valuable but, by itself, insufficient for effective decision making. Making better decisions requires wisdom. Wisdom is more than intelligence, knowledge or understanding. It means using these tools to think and act in ways which demonstrate sound judgement and which produce choices that are beneficial and productive.

> "Knowledge is of no value unless you put it into practice"
> Anton Chekhov

> "All truly wise thoughts have been thought already thousands of times; but to make them truly ours, we must think them over again honestly, till they take root in our personal experience."
> Goethe

You don't get wisdom out of a textbook. We can't get enough knowledge to make us wise. Wisdom is the effective use of knowledge. Wisdom involves the application of intelligence, knowledge, compassion, self-discipline and value principles to the decision-making process.

> "Wisdom is not a product of schooling, but of the lifelong effort to attain it."
> Albert Einstein

We attain wisdom by developing the expertise to deal with the difficult questions of life, and by adapting to its complex requirements. It involves determining the "right" thing to do and having the courage to do it. Our goal should be to become wise decision makers.

Acquire knowledge. Search for the truth. Develop and practice wisdom.

> "A good head and a good heart are always a formidable combination."
> Nelson Mandela

> "Honesty is the first chapter of the book of wisdom."
> Thomas Jefferson

BE MINDFUL

There are two elements to mindfulness: (1) being aware, being conscious of what is present, and what is going on around us, and (2) having the ability to concentrate, to focus on one thing, to give that one thing our undivided attention so we can deal with it most effectively.

> "The mind is just like a muscle – the more you exercise it, the stronger it gets and the more it can expand."
> Idowu Koyenikan

Awareness - You have probably observed people who seemed oblivious to what was going on around them, who were out of touch with reality. This condition is hardly conducive to making good choices. Circumstances matter, conditions matter, context matters, how the world really works (reality) matters. It means being conscious of everything that affects our interests, actions, goals, objectives and values. Being aware means being willing to confront reality, whether pleasant or unpleasant. Being aware means being conscious of, and respectful of, facts, reality and truth. To make better decisions, we need to learn to be aware, to embrace reality and then deal with it.

Awareness is a choice, and also a skill that can be developed. Awareness means being awake to the here and now. It is about being keenly observant of what is going on and why, of what is so, and why.

Understand that we control awareness like a dimmer switch on an electric light. We can willfully increase or decrease our sensitivity to our surroundings and what is going on. It is not practical to be 100% aware, 100% of the time. Our level of awareness is a choice. Context, the nature and importance of what is present and what is going on should determine where we set our "awareness switch". To operate effectively, we need to determine which things can be left on "automatic" and which things warrant our full attention.

> "Mindfulness means being awake. It means knowing what you are doing."
> Jon Kabat-Zinn

Mindfulness means "feeling" life as it happens around us and within us. When mindful, we see things we have not seen before and see things differently than we have seen them before.

Unfortunately many of us make important, sometimes life changing, decisions with little or no awareness of how those choices will change the shape and direction of our lives. We commit to actions without considering the consequences. Awareness is critical to effective decision making.

One of the characteristics of living mindfully is seeking to understand the reasons for our beliefs. Our actions are driven by our perceptions, of which we may or may not be aware. We need to consciously determine our ideas and values about: what is really important in life, how people should relate to one another, what is right and what is wrong, what is good and what is evil, what constitutes justice and what gives meaning to life. Critically examine your perceptions and ensure that they are really yours, not borrowed unconsciously from others.

Mindfulness is our basic tool for adapting to, and successfully coping with, reality.

Focus - Our minds naturally have a tendency to jump around from one subject to another like a monkey jumping from one branch to the next. Controlling what Buddhists refer to as our "Monkey Minds" is essential to rational thought and effective decision making. To "bind the monkey" we must understand our minds, our feelings and perceptions and learn to focus on one thing at a time.

> "Concentration is a cornerstone of mindfulness practice. Your mindfulness will only be as robust as the capacity of your mind to be calm and stable. Without calmness, the mirror of mindfulness will have an agitated and choppy surface and will not be able to reflect things with any accuracy."
> Jon Kabat-Zinn

Increase Mindfulness - Fortunately, we can learn to be mindful. Like any life skill, it takes time and effort. The first, and essential, step is to decide that you <u>want</u> to learn to be mindful.

To make better decisions, to make changes, to make improvements, the starting point is awareness. Pay attention. Be "present". When walking a path in the woods, notice the leaves, the weeds, the bark on the trees, the wildlife, the patterns created by sunlight sifting through the canopy. When walking a city street, notice the varying architecture of buildings, the cars passing, and especially the people. When participating in a meeting, observe: not only the content, but the ongoing "process". What does the body language of participants indicate? What role is authority playing in the meeting? What "hidden agendas" are being served? Be observant.

When dealing with a problem or issue, concentrate on concentrating. When your mind strays, gently bring it back to the subject at hand. Focus on your written definition of the issue. It will help you concentrate. Jot down your thoughts. It will help you concentrate.

The "Law of Cause and Effect" asserts that for every effect there is a cause. When you observe an effect, think about and identify the possible causes.

Many practitioners, myself included, contend you can train your mind to be more mindful through the practice of meditation. Thich Nhat Hanh defines mindfulness as "keeping one's consciousness alive to the present reality". He contends that meditation that focuses on one's breathing is a useful process for training the mind to be mindful, to become more aware and to increase the ability to focus. When we practice mindfulness in order to build up concentration, mindfulness is like a seed. Properly tended, it grows. Mindfulness frees us of forgetfulness and dispersion and makes it possible to live fully each moment of life. Hanh suggests that "Whenever your mind becomes scattered, concentrate on your breathing as the means to take hold of your mind again."

To learn more about improving mindfulness through meditation, read *THE MIRACLE OF MINDFULLNESS* by Thich Nhat Hanh.

> "Training your mind to be in the present moment is the #1 key to making **healthier choices.**"
> Susan Albers

One of the basic tenants of mindfulness is living in the here and now. Not worrying about yesterday or tomorrow, but being fully alive to, and conscious of, the present. Pope John XXIII elaborated on this short term focus in a treatise entitled JUST FOR TODAY:

> **"Just for today,
> I will try to live for this day alone,
> Without wishing to solve my life's problems all at once.**
>
> **Just for today,
> I will take care of how I present myself: I will dress simply;
> I will not raise my voice.
> I will be polite in my manners; I will not criticize anyone;
> I will not look to improve or discipline anyone other than myself.**
>
> **Just for today,
> I will be happy in the certainty that I was created to be happy,
> not only in the world to come, but also in this one**
>
> **Just for today,
> I will adapt to circumstances, without expecting circumstances to adapt to my wishes.**

Just for today,
I will devote ten minutes of my time to sitting in silence
and listening to God,
remembering that, just as food is necessary for the life of
the body,
so silence and listening are necessary for the life of the
soul.

Just for today,
I will do a good deed and tell no one about it.

Just for today,
I will do at least one thing that I do not enjoy, and if my
feelings are hurt,
I will make sure no one notices.

Just for today,
I will make a plan: perhaps I will not follow it perfectly, but
still I will make it.
And I will guard against two obstacles, haste and
indecision.

Just for today,
I will know from the bottom of my heart, no matter how it
will seem,
that God cares for me like no one else in this world.

Just for today,
I will have no fears. In particular, I will not be afraid to
enjoy what is beautiful and to believe in love.

I can easily do for twelve hours, what I would find
daunting if I had to do for a lifetime."

Not a bad mantra by which to live our lives - just for today!

DEVELOP LIFE GOALS AND OBJECTIVES

To determine how to live, we must first determine that for
which we are living. Defining clear personal goals and
objectives keeps us focused on who we want to be and what we

want to accomplish. Goal setting is the first step in turning the intangible into the tangible. Our most important goals and objectives are those which define the kind of person we want to be.

> "People with goals succeed because they know where they're going."
>
> Earl Nightingale

Stephen Covey, in *The 7 Habits of Highly Effective People*, phrases it as: "Begin With the End in Mind", i. e. start with a clear idea of your destination, your goals and objectives. To help us get started, he suggests that we all complete the following exercise:

> "See yourself going to the funeral of a loved one. As you enter the funeral parlor or chapel, you see the faces of friends and family. You feel the shared sorrow of losing someone important, the joy of having known the deceased, which radiates from the hearts of the people around you. As you walk to the front of the room and look into the casket, you come face to face with yourself. This is your funeral. All of these people have come to honor you, to express feelings of love and appreciation for your life.
>
> The program in your hand indicates that there are to be four speakers, the first from your immediate family, the second a close friend, someone who can relate who you were as a person, the third is an associate with whom you worked for a long time and the fourth is someone from your church or other organization where you were involved in service.
>
> Now think deeply. What would you like for them to have seen in you? What contributions, what

achievements would you want them to remember? Look carefully at the people around you. What difference would you have liked to have made in their lives?"

Think carefully about what you want those closest to you to think and say about you. Start right now living a life consistent with the values that will enable, those who care about you, (and especially to enable you), to truthfully understand that you made a positive difference in people's lives.

Goals - are statements (decisions) about what we want from life. Our goals should include statements about the kind of person we want to be (I want to be a good father), what we want to accomplish (I want to write a book about making life-shaping decisions), and what we want to experience (I want to visit all the US National Parks). Goals are longer term and more general than objectives. Goals should establish the direction and parameters for our lives. Goals should incorporate our values. When determining goals, it is useful to test them against our statements of values, and vice versa, to assure that they are consistent. Inconsistencies may warrant modifications to one or the other. That's ok. Inconsistencies aren't. Goals should reflect what we love, what is really important to us.

Objectives - define results to be accomplished in specific, measurable terms, with specified due dates. Always ask: what are the end results that I want? The attainment of objectives provides the building blocks for the accomplishment of goals. Objectives are end results to be achieved within a certain period of time. To be effective determinants of personal accomplishments, goals and objectives must be integrated, i.e. they must be consistent and mutually supportive. The attainment of objectives must lead to the accomplishment of goals, which, in turn, fulfill your personal purpose.

Examples of goals and objectives that illustrate the distinction between them:

Goal: I want to be a good father.

> Related Objective: Starting this weekend, I will plan and engage in an activity with Joey, every weekend, for an uninterrupted duration of at least 2 hours.

> Related Objective: I will read to Joey every evening.

Goal: I want to help relieve life's burdens for those less fortunate.

> Related Objective: By the end of this month I will select a social services agency to which I will commit at least six hours of effort every month.

Goals and objectives are not just for businesses. It is useful to think about goals and objectives in each area of your life:

- Family
- Physical & Health
- Career
- Spiritual
- Moral & Ethical
- Financial
- Mental & Educational

It is imperative to write down your goals and objectives. Writing forces us to think about and clarify our targets. It also increases the probability that we will reach our goals. Various research studies have found that those who write their goals and objectives are from three to nine times as likely to achieve them as those who don't. Whether the most accurate multiplier is three or nine is not important. The fact is that writing them significantly increases the probability of achieving them. **WRITE THEM DOWN!**

> "You control your future, your destiny. What you think about, comes about. By recording your dreams and goals on paper, you set in motion the process of becoming the person you most want to be. Put your future in good hands – your own."
>
> Mark Victor Hansen

Some other guidelines for developing goals and objectives:

- **Personalize** - Assure that your goals are things you really want, not just statements designed to impress someone. Goals are personal. Make them yours.
- **Be Specific** - Make your goal and objective statements definitive. Identify exactly what you want in as much detail as possible.
- **Be Realistic** – Goals and objectives should be attainable. They should require stretch but be possible. The right amount of stretch is a tough call. You should be looking for the right balance of challenge and reason. Many err on the side of aiming too low. We tend to underestimate our potentials. However, consistently missing unrealistically high targets can frustrate and discourage. Construct some goals you are reasonably certain of attaining. Success builds confidence and confidence generates more success.
- **Measure** - Find a way to make goals and objectives measurable. Not all will be quantifiable. Use numbers if you can, but if numbers don't fit, find another yardstick. It's hard to put a number on attaining a specific diploma, degree, certificate or license, but when you hold the document with your name on it in your hand

you know you've accomplished something. Measurements are important for indicating when you've hit your target, and equally important, for indicating progress. Use measurement to determine if you are really spending time on the things you have identified as important.

- **Use Benchmarks** - For long term goals, establish benchmarks (shorter term targets) to measure progress.
- **Be Positive** - Write goal and objective statements in the positive rather than the negative. Use positive words like *achieve*, *become* and *obtain* instead of *avoid, reduce* or *less*. Instead of declaring that you want to reduce the time you spend watching TV, state that you intend to read at least 18 thought provoking books per year. Instead of saying "I want to lose 13 pounds", say "I want to achieve a weight of 175 lbs. and be able to run a mile in 8 minutes by May 31".
- **Be Consistent** – Be sure that your goals are not conflicting or mutually exclusive. Test them against each other. If your goal is to be a social worker, it is not likely that you can realistically expect to live in an 18 room mansion with an ocean view, (unless you have another source of wealth).
- **Set Dates** -Your targets should be time specific. Goals are typically long term and include what you want to be, so target dates can be more nebulous. Objectives should each have a clear target date for attainment.
- **Focus** – Attainment is significantly dependent upon focused attention and effort. Problems with achievement can often be traced to lack of focus. Few of us can effectively pursue fifteen objectives simultaneously. Prioritize and then stagger target dates to assure that attainment is realistic. Then really concentrate on a few high priorities.

- **Share Selectively** – Goals and objectives are personal. Wide distribution invites expressions of skepticism and unreliable advice. Share them only with one to three persons whose advice you trust and ask those persons to periodically review progress with you and hold you accountable.
- **Review** – Keep goal and objective statements visible and review them periodically, (at least once or twice a month. For maximum effectiveness, internalize them to the extent that they are a part of your consciousness for automatic reference when making serious decisions.

The most important benefit of setting and writing down goals doesn't come from the attainment of the goals, but from the self – awareness, discipline and priorities established by going through the process. Taking goal and objective setting seriously can make a positive difference in one's life, and testing decisions against goals and objectives can help one make significantly better decisions.

We seldom have the opportunity to go back and make a new start, but we can start right now to construct a new ending.

Aim high when selecting goals. Consider not only the results you want but also the price you are willing to pay to achieve those results. We must realistically assess the effort, sacrifices and the tradeoffs necessary to realize a particular dream. High personal costs should not automatically dissuade one from pursuing a goal. Just be sure you understand the price and are willing to pay it.

> "When we are motivated by goals that have deep meaning, by dreams that need completion, by pure love that needs expressing, then we truly live."
> Greg Anderson

Goals and objectives clarify purpose and increase our capacity to accomplish.

Developing goals and objectives is important to the accomplishment of any endeavor, but merely developing them is not the end. Having established goals and objectives, it is imperative to ask: what do I have to know and learn to achieve them? How do I learn what I need to know? What do I have to <u>do</u> to achieve them? Without the required knowledge and a plan of action, goals become wishes with little chance of realization.

When making important decisions, always consider whether a course of action enhances or impedes your ability to achieve your goals and objectives.

<u>USE TIME WISELY</u>

Time is our most precious resource and time decisions are among the most important decisions we make. We make decisions all day, every day, about how we are going to use our time. We may ask ourselves: "what am I going to do: today? this morning? for the next hour? for the next ten minutes?", or we may not consciously ask these critical questions and just let time slide. Remember that a decision NOT to decide is still a decision. How you answer these questions affects the quality of your life. When you are asked to do something, or decide to do something, that requires a commitment of your time, understand the commitment is for a piece of your life. Recognize that your time = your life. Ask yourself if playing time-devouring video games or watching mind-numbing TV is really how you want to spend your <u>life</u>.

> "Dost thou love life? Then do not squander time, for that's the stuff life is made of."
> Benjamin Franklin

When thinking about time, think not about saving time, but "Making Time" for things that matter. Make a list of the distractions, (junk emails, social media, videos, etc.) that steal your time every day. Identify ways to eliminate those thieves from your agenda. At the end of each day, or the first thing in the morning, select two or three significant tasks for the day. Write them down. Schedule one or more times to work on those tasks. Lock out the distractions. Focus during those times. Get the tasks done.

This is not to imply we should work all the time. Everyone needs to spend time having fun, learning, exercising, spiritually recharging and just relaxing. Just be conscious of the importance of time and <u>intentional</u> about how you use it.

Time is almost always an important element of decision making. We often do not have the time to gather and analyze all the information we would like before a decision must be made. How you use the time that is available is important. When framing the issue that requires a decision, identify the time when you want to make your choice, and schedule backwards from there, so you can give the decision the time and effort you decide it warrants.

Don't procrastinate! The bane of effective decision making is putting off working at the issue until there is insufficient time for careful analysis and reflection, and/or some good options are no longer available. Hasty decisions about important issues are often lousy decisions. Take control of the process. Start early and give yourself enough time to do it right.

> "This time, like all times, is a very good one, if we but know how to use it."
> Ralph Waldo Emerson

LEARN TO LEARN

Be a learner. No matter how it turns out, every experience has something to teach us. Reflect on your major decisions and the consequences. In anticipation of an experience, contemplate: "what should I learn from this?" After each experience, ask yourself "what did I learn from that?"

> "Live your life as though you were to die tomorrow. Learn as if you were to live forever."
> Mahatma Gandhi.

Develop a learning mindset. Learn to learn. It is a skill that can be developed and improved. Develop an interest in acquiring knowledge. Ask lots of questions; to yourself and to others. Learning is more than schooling. It is a state of mind, a willingness to consciously look at the world and life with a deep sense of curiosity and wonder. View learning as something delightful. Seek mentors and teachers who can help with the process.

> "Always walk through life as if you have something new to learn, and you will."
> Vernon Howard

With a learning mindset, setbacks are not failures. They become data that can be framed into opportunities to learn, to improve. The first time a child touches a hot stove, the child learns something. That information is stored in a data bank that is useful for shaping future decisions. Every experience has that potential, but the process is much more effective if we make a conscious effort to learn from our experiences.

One of the ultimate purposes of life is to learn. Learning gives life meaning and helps us understand life's meaning. Learning enables more effective decision making. Life is a school, complete with tests. The tests can help us learn what we need to learn.

Deliberately expose yourself to new experiences, ideas, information and opinions. Consciously and continuously strive to be more aware, more knowledgeable and more understanding of everything that is relevant to you. Learning can be fun, not a chore, if you **decide** it is fun. Life will be more interesting and exciting if you are constantly learning.

Our lives are shaped largely by the decisions we make. The more skills we develop, (like problem solving skills, human relations skills, etc) and the more knowledge we acquire (about things like: how the world works, why people act the way they do, etc), the better our decisions will be, and the better the quality of our lives will be.

Learn from experience. Doing the same thing over and over and expecting different results is one of the definitions of insanity. Doing *more* of what doesn't work, does not work. Focus on what does work and do more of that. When traditional solutions don't work, create new approaches to try.

Writing can help us learn. In high school and college I strongly disliked writing courses. In graduate school, I was forced to write more and got better at it, but still didn't particularly like it. Since, I have learned the wisdom of this observation:

> "Learning to write is learning to think. You don't know anything clearly unless you can state it in writing."
> S. I. Hayakawa

I love to learn and have learned to like to write.

Learn from mistakes. We all make them. Don't let mistakes discourage you. They are opportunities to learn. Admit them. Examine the "why". Reflect on the lessons learned. Keep an open mind. Make adjustments. Try again, or try something else. The critical thing is to learn from the experience.

The world and life are constantly changing. To cope, to thrive, we must adapt. To remain adaptive, we must be committed to a life of continuous learning.

> "The capacity to learn is a *gift.*
> The ability to learn is a *skill*.
> The willingness to learn is a *choice*"

Brian Herbert

Curiosity - Consciously strive to develop a healthy curiosity. It is a trait that can be developed, and can broaden knowledge and perspectives. Try new experiences. Explore new places. Ask "why" questions. Curiosity generates energy, gets us involved in life, facilitates learning, uncovers opportunities and adds to the quality of our lives. A prime driver of learning is the search for answers to life's questions. The questions that engage our minds reflect our interests and influence the direction and quality of our lives. Curiosity can be developed if one has the desire and the discipline to work at it. Michael Gelb, in his book; *How to Think Like Leonardo da Vinci,* suggests that we:

- Keep a journal
- Jot down ideas, impressions and observations as they occur.
- In your notebook, make a list of 100 questions that you think are important.
- Review your list and choose the 10 that seem most significant.
- Rank the ten in order of importance to you.
- Set aside a time to contemplate the first question on your list.

- Explore the alternatives, look for themes and relationships, concentrate, until you are satisfied that you have a valid answer.
- Repeat with each question.

Develop an insatiable curiosity. The continuous quest for learning is a powerful force.

LEARN TO LISTEN!

The most useful skill to learn for dealing effectively with people is the skill of listening, really LISTENING. Real listening can't happen unless you have a sincere desire to understand what you're hearing, and that's not an easy task to manage. Real listening requires intention, concentration and effort. Listening may seem like giving up power because you are not in control of the conversation. In fact, it enhances the probability of effective outcomes. "When you stop preaching and really listen, here's what happens" (from *The 7 Habits of Highly Effective People, by Stephen Covey)*

- **People are more willing to trust you**. If you don't have people's trust, you will never be able to influence them.
- **You acquire useful information**, which makes it much easier to find solutions.
- **You gain insight into other people's perceptions** and what it will take to make a solution acceptable to them.
- **You begin to see other people as individuals – and maybe even allies.** Together, you move from I/they to US.
- **You can develop solutions that other people are willing to accept and even support.** When people contribute to the solutions, become co-owners, they are more likely to commit and follow through.

- **When people feel heard, they are more willing to listen.** If people do not feel that you "get" them, they are not inclined to expend the effort to listen to and understand you.

This is not to say that listening guarantees a favorable outcome every time, but failure to listen usually guarantees the outcome will not be optimal, and it may be a complete failure.

In *The 7 Habits,* Covey refers to this skill as "empathic listening", and urges us to "Seek First to Understand and then to be Understood".

He indicates that "next to physical survival, the greatest need of a human being is to be understood, to be affirmed, to be validated, to be appreciated. Listening with empathy to another person provides that person with psychological 'air'. Once *that* need is met, you can move on to problem solving or influencing." If that need is not first met, the person will be too preoccupied with "gasping for air" to appreciate the wisdom of your solutions. He is not likely to listen to you until you have listened to him.

LEARN to listen. It's amazing what you will LEARN. LISTEN to learn, not to frame your reply. Take time to listen, to others and to the still, small voice inside. Your unconscious often has something useful to convey.

READ

> "The more you read, the more things you will know.
> The more you know, the more places you'll go".
> Dr. Suess

Experiences enhance our ability to make effective decisions and cope with challenges. They enrich our lives. We should seek out and take advantage of opportunities to create and embrace positive personal experiences. But, there is a practical limit to what we can personally experience. There is simply not enough time to learn, through experiences, what we need to learn. There is a much broader scope of wisdom available, if we include learning from what others have written about experiences and what they learned from them, whether fact or fiction. It's a cliché, but true, that those who don't read are no better off than those who can't. There is much to read and we must be selective. There is a lot of junk written. To develop wisdom it is important to reflect on the thoughts of the world's wisest thinkers.

> "Employ your time in improving yourself by other men's writings so that you shall come easily by what others labored hard for."
> Socrates

Reading can take us to worlds we will never see and helps us understand and learn from people of cultures we will never encounter. It enables us to travel instantly through distance and time, to understand our origins, our heritage and the lessons of history. It helps us understand how the world works and why people act the way they do. It stretches our minds and helps us see the world in new ways. It increases our sensitivity to people and to nature. Reading prepares us for life and changes lives. Reading can help us understand how to be better human beings.

> "No matter how busy you think you are, you must find time for reading, or surrender yourself to self-chosen ignorance."
> Atwood H. Townsend

> "Reading is everything. Reading makes me feel like I've accomplished something, learned something, become a better person. Reading makes me smarter.

Reading gives me something to talk about. Reading is escape, and the opposite of escape. It's a way to make contact with reality. It's a way of making contact with someone else's imagination. Reading is grist. Reading is bliss."

Nora Ephron

"What an astonishing thing a book is. It's a flat object made from a tree with flexible parts on which are imprinted lots of funny dark squiggles. But one glance at it and you're inside the mind of another person, maybe somebody dead for thousands of years. Across the millennia, an author is speaking clearly and silently inside your head, directly to you. Writing is perhaps the greatest of human inventions, binding together people who never knew each other, people of distant epochs. Books break the shackles of time. A book is proof that humans are capable of working magic."

Carl Sagan

DEVELOP COMPETENCE

Select a skill, a task, a hobby, or sport that interests you and choose to become competent at it, not perfect, not necessarily excellent, but competent. You do not have to be the "best" at anything, but it is important that you <u>do your best</u> at things that matter to you. Noting improvement from personal effort, developing competence, builds confidence and self- esteem.

VIEW THE SITUATION FROM THE OTHER PERSON'S PERSPECTIVE

It can be difficult to be objective and rational about a situation in which you are emotionally involved. It can be useful to mentally remove yourself from the decision and treat the situation as if a friend had described the circumstances and asked you for advice. This process may help you more readily see the situation from multiple perspectives and to be creative in thinking about alternatives and win-win solutions.

CONTROL THE WAY YOU TALK TO YOURSELF

We all talk to ourselves constantly. Make the tone of those conversations positive, not critical or negative. Don't beat yourself up for mistakes or shortcomings. Don't delude yourself about reality, but focus on accomplishments and successes. Understand your feelings, but focus on your behavior. You feel the way you feel because of what you do. If you want to change how you feel, change what you are doing. Anger and fear are major impediments to rational decision making. Talk with yourself about your anger and fears. Ask yourself how you would like to act if you were not angry or afraid.

BE ADAPTABLE

The world changes constantly, circumstances change, our understanding changes. We have to adapt to keep up, and to grow. Being willing to concede that one is wrong, mistaken or unknowing is not demonstrating weakness, but strength. The attitude of a wise Roman Emperor indicates the way we should think.

> "If someone is able to show me that what I think or do is wrong, I will happily change, for I seek the truth, by which no one ever was truly harmed."
> Marcus Aurelius

We should embrace change, learn from it and grow with it. Be willing to change to make things work.

> "The only way that we can live, is if we grow. The only way that we can grow is if we change. The only way

that we can change is if we learn. The only way we can learn is if we are exposed. And the only way that we can become exposed is if we throw ourselves out into the open. Do it. Throw yourself."
C. JoyBell

Sometimes adapting means acceptance. There are some things we just cannot change. In those cases it is necessary to heed the wisdom of the Serenity Prayer:

> "God give me the serenity to accept those things I cannot change, courage to change the things I can, and wisdom to know the difference."

BE PERSISTENT

Not all of your choices will turn out to be good ones. Not everything you try will succeed. YOU WILL FAIL! (That's a good thing). It's not just OK, it's essential.

"Failing isn't bad when you learn what not to do."
Albert Einstein

Those who excel at whatever they do have learned to learn from failures. The excellent fail more often than the mediocre. They begin more. They attempt more. They succeed because they have failed more and learned from their failures.

> "I do not think that there is any other quality so essential to success of any kind as the quality of perseverance. It overcomes almost everything."
> D. Rockefeller

It is only from the experience of challenging ourselves that we learn and grow, and we often mature and learn more from our failures than from our successes. When we put ourselves on the line, when we fall down and get up again, we become stronger and more resilient.

"Don't let what you cannot do interfere with what you can do."

John Wooden

You will fail. It will never be particularly pleasant. The key is to learn from the process. Consciously reflect on the process and ask: "what did I learn that will be of benefit for my next experience?" Mistakes and failures are proof that you are trying and that's a good thing.

Failure does not have to be an end point. If a goal is worthy, and an approach did not work, and if you learned from the experience, trying again with a modified approach is a viable option.

"PRESS ON

Nothing in the world can take the place of persistence. Talent will not; nothing is more common than unsuccessful people with talent. Genius will not; unrewarded genius is almost a proverb. Education alone will not; the world is full of educated derelicts. Persistence and determination alone are omnipotent."

Anonymous

I have had the above quote on my wall for years and found its truth apparent in multiple instances.

"A failure is not always a mistake. It may simply be the best one can do under the circumstances. The real mistake is to stop trying"

B. F. Skinner

"Through perseverance many people win success out of what seemed destined to be certain failure."
Benjamin Disraeli

"How much you can learn when you fail determines how far you will go in achieving your goals."
Roy Bennett

We do not need to be perfect nor measure our worth by the standards of others. We do not have to make overnight giant strides in productivity. We should just strive to become a little better every day. We can take pride and comfort in whatever we do if we understand that we have done our best.

> "The real contest, of course, is striving to reach your personal best, and that is totally under your control. When you achieve that, you have achieved success. Period! You are a winner and only you fully know if you have won."
> John Wooden

ESCAPE ESCAPISM

Ignoring or running away from problems only leads to more problems. The way to fix problems, whether they are the results of your choices or the choices of others, is to make new and better choices. You can't escape life or yourself. Deal with it.

PART V. HOW MIGHT I IMPROVE THE OUTCOMES OF MY DECISIONS?

Following a rational process can help us make better decisions. An effective decision-making process should satisfy the following criteria:

- It focuses on the <u>real</u> issues and needs.
- It encourages the gathering of relevant data.
- It is logical and widely applicable.
- It encourages the weighing of less-tangible considerations, such as values, goals and objectives, as well as facts.
- It encourages thoroughly thinking through alternatives, and possible consequences for the decision maker and for others.
- It urges timely action.

The proposed process incorporates twelve elements:

1. FRAME THE ISSUE
2. IDENTIFY THE INFORMATION NEEDED TO MAKE A GOOD DECISION
3. IDENTIFY VIABLE OPTIONS/ALTERNATIVES
4. CONSIDER THE LIKELY CONSEQUENSES / RESULTS
5. CONSIDER THE IMPACT ON OTHERS
6. TEST THE ALTERNATIVES AGAINST YOUR VALUES
7. TEST THE ALTERNATIVES AGAINST YOUR GOALS AND OBJECTIVES
8. TUNE IN TO YOUR INTUITION
9. THINK IT THROUGH
10. MAKE A DECISION
11. IMPLEMENT IT
12. CONDUCT POSTMORTEMS

While the proposed process is laid out in sequence, recognize that, to be most effective, it should be viewed as iterative. It is often beneficial to "loop back", to rethink previous conclusions as you employ the process. As you gather information you may see the need to redefine the issue. As you consider the consequences of your list of alternatives, you may realize that none of the consequences are acceptable, and thus you need a new list of options. At any point in the process you may have an "aha moment", in which you see things more clearly. The solution may become obvious or you may find it useful to backtrack and proceed from an earlier point in the process.

1. FRAME THE ISSUE

What's it about? The first step in the decision-making process is to define or "frame" the issue. I use the word *issue* advisedly. Much of what is written about decision making equates decision making with problem solving. While problem solving requires effective decision-making skills, not all decisions involve problems. The word "problem" has a negative connotation not always useful to the process. Choosing between alternative job offers, both significantly better than your current job, is not a problem. Choosing which of two good used cars to buy, is not a problem. View decisions, not as problems, but as opportunities of two types: the opportunity to make the best of the issue at hand, and the opportunity to practice, (and thus improve), your decision-making skills. Defining the essence and scope of the issue is the foundation of a useful process.

Framing involves answering some basic questions:

- Why is a decision required?
- What is the real issue?
- What are the root causes of the issue/problem?
- How important is the decision?

- What are the real needs associated with the decision?
- What is your primary objective? What are your secondary objectives?
- What are the primary, real constraints?
- What are your wants/preferences associated with the decision?
- By when should the decision be made?

Why? - Identifying why a decision is required helps define the issue and assists with answering other framing questions. "My boss told me that he wants my recommendation by Monday", is a legitimate reason for seeking an effective resolution and also establishes a deadline. Because I need reliable transportation to get to work, and "my mechanic just told me my vehicle won't last long", drives the need for a decision about transportation. Understanding the reason for making the decision will help you make better decisions.

What Is The Real Issue? - Issues sometimes wear disguises. Following an effective process to the ideal solution for the wrong issue is not productive. Definition is critical. The way you define an issue can significantly influence your choices. The question "should I buy the Sony or Samsung big screen TV?" might more legitimately be framed as "should I make such a purchase at all?"

What is the Root Cause? - If the issue is not a problem, why did it come up? If it is a problem, what is the root cause (or causes)? It is sometimes useful to utilize the elementary technique of asking: Why, Who, What, Where, When, and How.

When analyzing an issue or problem, it is useful to keep in mind the Pareto Principle (the 80/20 rule), which indicates that 80% of problems are the result of 20% of the causes, and that

80% of the benefits can be achieved by completing 20% of the solution elements. (Google - Pareto Principle).

How Important Is The Decision? - A fundamental issue is deciding how much time and effort to invest in a decision, how rigorously to apply the chosen process. The more critical the consequences, the more you should invest in the effort. To facilitate that process, a system that assigns a numerical ranking can be useful:

1   Paramount - These are the life-altering decisions that deserve our best efforts. (career choices, spouse choices, addictive substance choices, etc.).

2   Significant - These are the choices that have a major impact on the quality of our lives, but are not likely to completely change it. (buy a home in the suburbs or rent an apartment in the city).

3   Material – These make a difference, but don't have a major impact. (choosing a dude ranch or a beach resort for the next family vacation).

4   Mundane – These are the trivial choices we make every day. (what to have for lunch, which shoes to put on). They do not deserve a rigorous application of the process because the consequences don't matter much.

What Are The Real Needs? - Distinguish between wants and needs. What results are really necessary to solve the problem or resolve the issue? Needs are basic. They represent what is required. The key is focus. For the best results, focus on the real needs. The more clearly you see the results you need, the easier it will be to identify and evaluate choices, and thus make an effective decision.

What Are Your Objectives? - Objectives should address the real needs. They define results you wish to accomplish in specific, measurable terms, with specified due dates. Aristotle said "People are like archers. They need a clear target at which to aim". Clearly stated objectives help us identify what information we need, channel the development of alternatives and provide standards against which to test potential choices. Multiple objectives are typical for major decisions. Prioritize objectives in terms of importance. Identify all your objectives, even those that conflict. You will need to address the conflicts in the analysis phase. Write down all you hope to accomplish by making this decision.

What Are The Real Constraints? – Typically there are factors that limit the range of feasible choices. Money is a common constraint. A cap on the dollars available can limit the options. Time and geography can narrow the list of practical alternatives. Determine which constraints are *real*. Question every identified constraint to determine if it is in fact restrictive or simply a "mental" barrier, a factor of limited vision. Brainstorm how constraints might be removed, or rendered inconsequential.

What Are Your Wants/Preferences? - As humans, our emotions are real and relevant. That's ok. Making good decisions sometimes means resolving conflicts between wants and needs and thus requires tough choices. We should distinguish needs from wants, but it is unwise to treat decision making so mechanically that you ignore your emotions or the emotions of those affected by the decision. It is better to consciously acknowledge and consider your personal feelings and their impact on your choices than to have them unconsciously bias your thinking.

When? - Time is often a critical factor, sometimes imposed by others or by circumstances. Identify precisely when a decision must be made. Hard decisions deserve ample time for analysis. Allow sufficient time to utilize the process when dealing with important decisions. When circumstances permit, take control of the schedule and allow enough time to prepare for making the choice. Don't procrastinate until time pressures force you into making a poor or less than optimal choice. Putting off the analysis and the decision can mean that some attractive alternatives are no longer available or that someone else makes the decision for you. Set yourself a deadline.

Time and effort spent accurately defining/framing the decision issue will save time in the long run and provide a firm foundation for improving the quality of your decisions. Be thorough in defining the issue. Restate it in a number of different ways, until you are confident that you have it right. The best resolution to the wrong issue is not very helpful.

Writing down your issue definition is critical. It forces you to think it through. A "Framing Worksheet" to help with defining the scope of the decision issue is shown in Appendix A.

> "The formulation of a problem is often more essential than its solution."
>
> Albert Einstein

2. <u>IDENTIFY AND GATHER RELEVANT INFORMATION</u>

Once you have the issue clearly defined, ask yourself: "what information would be useful for making this decision?". Make a list of what you really need. For important decisions, it would be unusual for you to have in your memory bank everything necessary for making an effective decision. Additional information is usually required. Information is of three kinds: CRITICAL – information without which the decision should not be made (if at all possible), USEFUL – information it would be beneficial to have, if time permits, and IRRELEVANT – all information that has no impact on the decision. It is important to distinguish among the three types, to give priority to the critical and to refuse to spend time chasing the irrelevant.

> "The art of being wise is the art of knowing what to overlook."
>
> William James

Relevant information can be "hard", i. e. facts and figures, and "emotional" – how you feel about the issue and why you feel that way. Both are important. Don't ignore either. It is especially useful to ask yourself why you feel the way you do about a subject. What is the source of your feelings? Consider how those affected by the decision are likely to feel about the issue. That nagging feeling may be your conscience telling you "something is not right here".

There are myriad sources of information: books, articles, the internet, experts (authorities respected in their fields) and personal observation/experience. Use them. Whenever possible and practical, verify what you read or hear before giving it credibility.

Be selective. Do not accumulate data for the sake of data or to put off having to make the decision. Develop, refine and use your list of what you really need.

> "It is of the highest importance in the art of detection to be able to recognize, out of a number of facts, which is incidental and which vital"
>
> Sherlock Holmes (Arthur Conan Doyle)

Know when to quit! Deadlines may dictate, but so should judgement. Time spent on gathering information should be related to the importance of the decision. So always consider the "utility" of gathering additional information, i.e. at what point is the *value,* (improvement in the quality of the decision), of additional information insufficient to justify the *effort* to obtain more information? Keep asking yourself if more information will really enable you to make a more effective decision.

3. <u>IDENTIFY AND CLEARLY DEFINE ALTERNATIVES</u>

After gathering relevant information, it's time to consider potential alternatives. The decision you make can be no better than the best alternative you conjure up, so time spent identifying options is usually well spent. This is an important step. Far too many decisions are unsatisfactory because the decision maker failed to consider enough options. Ask yourself "what are the alternative ways that I might meet my objectives?"

- Brainstorm. Be creative. There are almost always more options than initially come to mind. Think outside the proverbial box.
- Don't evaluate options while creating. The key to brainstorming effectiveness is to suspend judgement when considering alternatives. Get as many options on the table as possible. Postpone critiquing to prevent stifling creativity.
- Examine your assumptions about limitations. Some constraints are real, but some are only mental. Imagine that the apparent limitation did not exist. What could you do then?
- Begin early and plan time for breaks in the process. Your subconscious will keep wrestling with the issue and may well come up with a fresh concept.
- Review your experience. What worked (or didn't work) for you in similar situations? You should learn from all experiences, but don't slip into the rut of considering just the same old alternatives.
- Aim high. Don't just settle for incremental improvements. Set lofty targets.
- Imagine what a person you admire and respect would do in your situation.

- Think for yourself first, and then seek suggestions from one or more persons you admire and respect. Sometimes the process of explaining the issue you are facing to someone else will stimulate you to come up with a new possibility. A different perspective can be helpful, but never abdicate the development of your alternatives list.
- Keep reviewing your list. Any one idea may spark a thought about a related possibility.
- Consider combining alternatives to develop one even better.

SCAMPER - is a creative thinking technique developed by Bob Eberle for use by school teachers. It can also be effective for developing additional ideas and concepts for resolving issues and solving problems. SCAMPER is an acronym of a process for identifying alternative solutions or resolutions:

Substitute: Replace some part of an identified option with something else.

Combine: Join two or more elements of an alternative resolution to come up with what could be a better alternative.

Adapt: Try changing various parts of a solution to create new alternatives.

Modify: Change various attributes of an issue to determine if doing so suggests possible resolutions. (attributes may include: color, shape, size, position, texture, etc.).

Purpose: Consider other uses for the subject. Think about other ways it could function to achieve different results.

Eliminate: Arbitrarily remove one or more elements of the issue or a solution and consider the impact.

Reverse: Change direction or orientation. Change/reverse the sequence of elements or steps.

MORPHOLOGICAL ANALYSIS - Fritz Zwicky, an astrophysicist who is credited with the discovery of what is referred to as dark matter, developed a process for systematically expanding the number of viable options to be considered when attempting to resolve a problem or issue. The process has been labeled "Morphological Analysis" or "Zwicky's Box." The steps of the process are as follows:

1. Carefully define/frame the issue.
2. Identify the relevant elements/parameters of the issue.
3. List the parameters across the top axis of a grid.
4. Under each parameter, list viable options for that parameter.
5. Hold one option of one parameter constant and consider combining it with each of the options in the other columns. Some combinations will be ridiculous, some untenable, but some may represent ideas with potential.
6. Discard those combinations that are impossible or unworkable. Add the viable ones to your list of alternatives for analysis.

Consider the following illustration:

Issue - Develop a new toy to add to the company product line.

PARAMETERS					
					Price
Theme	Target Age Group	Material	Color	Gender	Range
Space	3 to 5	Plastic	Red	Male	$5 to $10
Action	6 to 9	Wood	Blue	Female	$11 to $15
Animal	10 to 12	Metal	Green	Both	$16 to $20
Sports			Pink		$21 to $30
Cars			Yellow		
Party					

(OPTIONS)

Figure 1

The highlighted combination: an action toy for boys ages 10 to 12 made from blue plastic, priced in the $16 to $20 range, is one of several hundred that could be considered using the model. Looking at the various possible combinations may lead to concepts that would never have been considered otherwise.

Whatever process you use for generating alternatives, list all the options that have a reasonable chance of working. Thinking through a comprehensive list helps you avoid impulsively pursuing the first idea that sounds good, but may not be the best choice. Recognize that you cannot choose an alternative you have not included in the analysis, and your choice can be no better than the best of those on your list. Identify as many reasonable options as possible.

Think beyond the obvious parameters. Your alternatives should be driven by your objectives, but be sure your framing of the issue is appropriate. You may do a fantastic job of establishing and evaluating just the right alternatives for purchasing a new home in the ideal neighborhood, but if there is a reasonable probability that you will be transferred to another town in the next two years, renting should be included in your list of housing options.

Be very specific about defining the alternatives. Think them through and write them down.

4. CONSIDER THE CONSEQUENCES

No one has perfect foresight. It is difficult to predict the outcomes of possible choices. However, to make better decisions, you must make a conscious effort to predict the consequences of your choices. Carefully estimating the probable results of each of your options will help you select the one that best meets your objectives.

The more clearly you understand the issue, your objectives and the consequences of your options, the higher the probability your choice will be a good one. If you have accurately defined the consequences of your alternatives, your decision will sometimes become obvious, without further analysis.

Reflecting upon your careful definition of the issue and your specifically stated objectives:

1. Reject any that are clearly inferior. Refine your list of options to a manageable number, perhaps three to five. Winnowing out those inconsistent with real constraints can help narrow the list. Ranking, prioritizing can help as well.
2. Attempt to imagine the most likely implications of choosing each of these short list alternatives. Write them down. Be very realistic, specific, and accurate. Don't kid yourself.
3. Consider the long term impact of each option. Imagine how you would feel about the choice in a year, three years, ten years.
4. Use the hard data developed in your information search, but reflect on it with logic and judgement.
5. Identify and acknowledge uncertainties. You won't know the consequences for sure until after the decision.

6. Ask yourself: what has to happen or not happen for this situation to turn out well? What are the consequences of being wrong?
7. Ask yourself if you can live with what might realistically be a worst case scenario.
8. Consult with authorities you respect. A professional in the field (law, finance, medicine) may have a better grasp of the consequences of certain types of decisions than do you. For less technical issues, a trusted friend might serve as a sounding board.
9. Whenever possible, use scales that are objective, measurable, and meaningful and that reflect a reasonable level of precision for the subject being evaluated.
10. Narrow the list of options to those that come closest to meeting your objectives.
11. Developing an Option Comparison Matrix can be very helpful for comparing alternatives.

This approach involves selecting the criteria you consider important to a decision and then comparing alternatives using those criteria. Consider the following example of a family pondering the selection of a new home:

Criteria	Criteria Detail	Options		
		Oak Hill	Westridge	Maple
Home Size	Min 2,400 SF	2,800 SF	2,900 SF	2950 SF
	4 Bdrms	4	4	4
	3 Bth Rms	3	3	3
School Quality	Academic Perf	Ste Score 85	Ste Score 90	Ste Score 75
	Extracurricular	Very Good	Very Good	Good
Neighborhood Quality	Kid Friendly	Very Good	Excellent	Good
	Quiet	Good	Good	OK
Home Quality	Basic Structure	Very Good	Very Good	OK
	Amenities	Nice Extras	Nice Extras	Good
Yard Quality	Size	1/2 Acre	3/4 Acre	1 Acre
	Landscaping	Nice Shrubs, Grass	Nice trees, Shrbs, Flwers	Nice Trees, Grass
Mom Commute	< 35 Min	20 Min	25 Min	30 Min
Dad Commute	< 35 Min	30 Min	25 Min	20 Min
Basement	Full	Full	Full	Full
	Rec Area	Finshed	Could Be Fin	Could be Fin
Proximity to Retail	< 20 Min	15 Min	15 Min	20 Min
Purchase Price	< $350,000	$325,000	$335,000	$310,000

Figure 2

It treats all criteria equally. The value of the approach is that it forces you to think about what criteria are really important to you and it organizes the data in a way that facilitates the comparison of alternatives. It lends itself to inviting multiple participants to complete a worksheet and then compare worksheets to attempt to reach a consensus. The exercise can be a useful tool.

Probabilities - Many decisions deal with the future. The future is uncertain. Yet we constantly have to make decisions in the present, the results of which will depend on what <u>actually happens</u> in that uncertain future.

A helpful way of dealing with that conundrum is to think in terms of probabilities. Probability analysis involves assigning a meaningful numerical value to the likelihood that an event will happen in the future. There are at least two dimensions to probability. Mathematical probability involves the calculable prediction of outcomes from random actions or experiments. If you roll a six sided single die, the probability of any one of the numbers one to six coming up on top is 1/6 or 16.6667%. If you roll the die 1,000,000 times, each of the six numbers will come up pretty close to 16.67% of the time. Bayesian probability is a way of expressing, quantitatively, one's degree of belief or opinion that a certain thing will happen in the future. Most decisions do not involve six options with an equal probability of each occurring. You have to take the information you have, plus what you think you know and make a judgement about how likely it is that a particular thing will happen, or what the likely consequences of a choice might be. Getting your head around both these dimensions of probability will help you make better decisions. Assigning probabilities to future events and consequences will help you deal more effectively with the inevitable uncertainty. Just be sure you understand the difference and reliability of the two kinds of probabilities.

You are perhaps most frequently exposed to the concept of probabilities when you listen to a weather forecast. When that TV prognosticator states that there is a 70% chance of rain tomorrow, what she is really saying is "if conditions tomorrow are what we think they will be, there is a 70% probability those conditions will produce precipitation". Note that both dimensions of probability are involved. Meteorologists do not know what tomorrow's conditions will be. Based upon past weather patterns, what the patterns are today to the west, north, south and sometimes east, and what they know about the way weather behaves, they predict what they believe the conditions will be tomorrow. They are applying Bayesian probability, expressing a belief grounded in experience and knowledge. Based upon their study of the way weather has behaved in the past, the atmospheric conditions they expect for tomorrow have produced rain 7,000 out of the 10,000 times those conditions have occurred. They are applying mathematical probability.

To think about probabilities effectively, you need to understand these basics:

- The range of probabilities is always: 0% (cannot happen) to 100% (absolute certainty).
- The sum of the probabilities of all possible outcomes must be 100%, never more, never less.
- When using probabilities to express a quantitative degree of belief, you must include all the possible outcomes in the analysis. You cannot realistically assess the probability of any one outcome unless you consider all possible outcomes. Probabilities must always total 100%.
- If there are multiple <u>independent</u> ways an outcome might occur, the probability of the event occurring is equal to the probability of the way with the highest probability:
  - If in November you are assessing the probability of supplementing your nest egg by enough to make a down payment on a new car in March, and you identify the possible sources of funds and their probabilities as follows:

    You make enough profit from a garage sale - 15.00%
    you receive a year-end bonus at work - 40.00%
    your brother-in-law agrees to lend you the funds - 10.00%
    You hit the lottery - .0001%

Your probability of making that down payment is 40%, because that is the probability of the event that could trigger the outcome which has the highest probability of all the events that could trigger the outcome.

- The math is different if multiple events <u>must all</u> happen to trigger an outcome.

To determine the probability of two or more independent outcomes both/all happening, you multiply their individual probabilities together.

  o Assume you are assessing the possibility of an investment in a particular stock doubling in the next year. You estimate that in order for that to happen, three things must occur, and the probability of each of those three things happening is as follows:

  The total Stock Market must advance by at least 10%. Probability – 20%
  The company must beat the Analysts' earnings per share estimates by at least 20%. Probability – 25%
  The Federal Reserve must lower the discount rate by ¼ point. Probability – 20%
  The probability of all three things occurring and your stock doubling in value is: (20% X 25% = 5%) X 20% = 1%
  Note that the longer the "string" of independent occurrences that must materialize to produce a specific result, the lower will be the probability of that result.

Expected Value - Probabilities can help in dealing with decisions that have multiple, quantifiable consequences. The

Expected Value of a choice is the weighted average of the possible values of that outcome, where the weights used are the probabilities associated with each consequence. The Expected Value is the sum of: all possible outcomes multiplied by the probability that the outcome will occur.

Assume you have the opportunity to participate in a game of chance. This is a yes or no decision. It costs you $10 to participate. If you win, you get back your $10 plus varying amounts. After learning the rules, you calculate that the possible consequences and their associated probabilities are as follows:

1. You lose   – probability 60%
2. You win $10 – probability 25%
3. You win $20 – probability 10%
4. You win $50 – probability 5%

Do you play or not play?

Expected Value Table				
Consequence		Probability		Expected Value
Lose $10		0.60		-6.00
Win $10		0.25		2.50
Win $20		0.10		2.00
Win $50		0.05		2.50
Total Expected Value				$1.00

Figure 3

Note that this analysis does not tell you what decision to make. That might depend on how painful it would be for you to lose $10 at this time. It does not tell you what will happen if you play the game once. It does help you think rationally about the

119

decision. What it does tell you is that if you played this game 1,000 times, you would probably come out about $1,000 ahead.

To learn more about probabilities and their applications for decision making, read:

PROBABILITIES IN EVERYDAY LIFE by John D. McGervey.

5. CONSIDER THE IMPACT ON OTHERS

People Matter! - When considering the consequences of alternative decisions, pay particular attention to the consequences for others. Our decisions rarely affect only us. Think through who will be influenced by your decision and how they will be affected. Your choices can change lives, and not just your own. To help you understand the implications for others, write down the names of those likely to be impacted by your important decisions and the likely positive and negatives effects on their lives.

For many, a key life issue is finding the right balance between work and other activities, especially family life. If your family is important to you, your decisions should reflect that fact. Prioritize family in your time scheduling decisions. Demands on your time are infinite, but your time is finite. Make time for what is important to you.

Some decisions involve sacrifices. You may be perfectly willing to make personal sacrifices to take on and complete some task, because you value what you perceive to be the end result. Think carefully about the sacrifices others will have to make if you decide to pursue a particular course of action. Others who will be affected may not see the long term benefits that you see, or care as much about the outcome as you do. They may not be willing to make the sacrifices your decision will require of them.

Put yourself in the shoes of those who will be impacted by your choice. Treat them the way you would like to be treated.

When major decisions will impact others, get them involved in the process. Let them know what you are thinking. Share relevant information. Ask for, and listen to, input. Demonstrate a willingness to consider ideas and alternatives suggested by others. This does not mean that such decisions should always be made by consensus or majority vote. You should not abdicate decisions. Even if you have to make an unpopular decision, you will receive less resistance and more cooperation and commitment if those affected are informed and involved.

6. TEST POSSIBLE CHOICES AGAINST YOUR VALUES

Several years ago, Tony Campolo, a noted Christian author, who was the key speaker at a leadership conference I attended, related some research in which a group of mothers of Japanese children was asked: "if you could be granted one wish for your child, for what would you wish?" The overwhelming response from that group was that they would wish for their children to be "successful". When a group of American mothers was asked the same question, the overwhelming response was that they would wish for their children to be "happy". The question posed was a question about VALUES. Tony contended that both answers were inappropriate. What we should wish for our children is that they be "GOOD". Being good means owning and practicing the right values.

To determine if a decision is "right" for you, test possible choices against your values. To test a decision against your values, you must have previously considered and defined your ethical and moral standards and what core values are really important to you. That requires careful thought and is something that should be done with deliberation and great care, before you are faced with the pressure of making an important decision. By deciding <u>now</u> what is important to you, you will be better prepared to <u>align your actions with your values</u> in times of crisis or change.

Testing possible choices against your values should be viewed as a critical step in the decision making process.

7.   TEST POSSIBLE CHOICES AGAINST YOUR PERSONAL GOALS AND OBJECTIVES

Not all of your decisions will impact your personal goals and objectives. When one does, it is important to determine the likely implications each choice would have for their attainment. Of course, to test for implications, you must have defined your goals and objectives. If you haven't developed goals and objectives, DO IT NOW, before you have to make the next significant decision in your life.

No matter how expeditious a choice may appear in the short run, if it is inconsistent with where you want to go and what you want to be, it is not likely to be a wise choice.

When evaluating possible decision alternatives, ask yourself what impact that choice is likely to have on the attainment of your personal goals and objectives. Write down your goals and objectives, keep them available and consciously test alternatives against them. This practice becomes an effective means for weeding out unacceptable options and will help keep your life on track.

8. TUNE IN TO YOUR INTUITION

Intuition sometime gets a bad rap because it is 'unscientific". It smacks of "having a hunch about which horse to bet on in the fifth race". It is very important not to confuse hunches with hopes. Do not let what you would <u>like</u> to have happen determine what you think <u>will</u> happen.

In fact, intuition accurately defined and applied, can be a great asset for effective decision making. If intuition is understood as drawing on a synthesis of one's <u>experience</u>, <u>knowledge</u> and <u>values</u> when making decisions, it can be a very useful resource. Intuition can be viewed as using what you know. We sometimes do not realize what all we know. Noted psychologists Carl Jung and Rollo May both wrote of intuition as the unconscious mind delivering data and experiences to the conscious mind. Think of your unconscious mind combing through every relevant experience you have ever had, every relevant fact you have ever learned and every personal value you have established, and sending a summary by email to your conscious mind. Jung described intuition as "an unconscious ability to perceive possibilities, to see the global picture while addressing the local situation." So intuition can also include concepts of creativity and perspective.

If we have the right values and principles, and have learned the lessons of our experiences, doing what "feels right" can often be a useful guide to behavior.

If intuition is to be useful, you must be careful about the facts, experiences and values stored in your unconscious. Intuition will only be as good as the data that feeds it. The reliability of intuition can be enhanced through reflection and meditation.

Give your subconscious/intuition time to work. Start early and schedule intervals in your conscious effort. Ask yourself "What is my 'gut' telling me about this choice?"

This does not mean that analysis should be ignored. Gathering and analyzing relevant information is crucial. The best approach is to utilize both reasoning and intuition. Making the most effective choices requires both.

9. THINK IT THROUGH

This is the point in the process to analyze and evaluate alternatives. Start by reviewing all the previous steps and asking yourself fundamental questions:

- Is the issue adequately defined? Have I identified the real need?
- Are my objectives clearly defined and will attaining the objectives satisfy the real need?
- Is my assessment of the importance of the decision accurate?
- Have I identified the constraints accurately?
- Have I accurately described my personal feelings and preferences? Can I objectively assess their impact on the decision?
- Do I have the information required to make an effective decision?
- Have I creatively and realistically identified the alternatives?
- Have I adequately anticipated the consequences of each alternative?
- Have I adequately considered the impact of each alternative on other people?
- Have I adequately evaluated the consistency of each alternative with my values?
- Have I adequately evaluated the consistency of each alternative with my goals and objectives?
- If probabilities are involved in my analysis, have I included all possible options and realistically estimated probabilities?
- Have I objectively eliminated unacceptable alternatives?

Rigorously challenge each of the constraints. Are there ways to mitigate any of them? Reassess the alternatives. Has your work thus far stimulated the possibility of others? Would combining two or more result in a better alternative?

Be particularly sensitive to evidence that indicates an error in your thinking, and be willing to correct such errors. Thinking can change thinking. That is one of the attributes that makes it so powerful.

Make any refinements indicated by this review.

Establish the criteria by which you will evaluate the alternatives. This is an important process because it forces you to think about what is really important to you and what is really relevant to the decision at hand. Make sure that the criteria accurately reflect your values, goals and concerns for the impact on others

Next, apply sound reasoning to evaluate the alternatives and the anticipated consequences. There are a variety of ways to organize and view the alternatives to facilitate the evaluation.

One of the simplest is to list the alternatives with the associated pros and cons of each. You can then make a choice based upon your judgement of the best combination of pros and cons.

Another simple, but somewhat subjective method is to rank alternatives by conducting "matched pair comparisons":

List the alternatives in any order.

> Alternative 1
> Alternative 2
> Alternative 3
> Alternative 4
> Alternative 5

Compare alternatives 1 and 2. If 2 appears more effective than 1, move it ahead of 1. The list now looks like this:

Alternative 2
Alternative 1
Alternative 3
Alternative 4
Alternative 5

Repeat the process. Compare 3 to 1. If 3 looks better than 1, move it ahead of 1.

Compare 3 to 2. If 3 is better move 3 to the top of the list.

Continue the process until you have arranged in list in your perceived order of effectiveness. You may end up with a list that looks entirely different from the original:

Alternative 3
Alternative 2
Alternative 1
Alternative 5
Alternative 4

Not all pros and cons, and not all criteria, are created equal. Judgements based upon mentally attempting to combine criteria can get subjective. Weighting criteria can increase the probability of selecting the most effective alternative. A more precise and usually more useful approach is to:

1. Develop a list of decision criteria
2. Assign weights to the criteria on a scale of 1 to 10
3. Make judgements about how well each of the alternatives satisfies the criteria and assign a score from 1 to 100.
4. Arrange the data in a "Weighted Score Decision Matrix".

5. Multiply the raw scores by the weights
6. Add up the weighted scores
7. Consider the weighted total scores as a basis for making your choice.

The following is an illustration of how John might use this approach to evaluate job offers upon graduation:

WEIGHTED SCORE DECISION MATRIX		Job A		Job B		Job C		Job D	
CRITERIA	Weight	Raw Score	Wghted Score	Raw Score	Wghted Score	Raw Score	Wghted Score	Raw Score	Wghted Score
My "fit" with the people I've met	10	60	600	50	500	80	800	70	700
Quality/reputation of the company	9	50	450	40	360	80	720	30	270
Starting salary	6	50	300	80	480	60	360	70	420
Skills development/ Learning potential	8	80	640	70	560	85	680	40	320
Work schedule flexibility	4	70	280	55	220	90	360	35	140
Opportunity for advancement	7	65	455	90	630	75	525	55	385
Benefits	3	80	240	60	180	65	195	70	210
Total Wghted Score			2965		2930		3640		2445

Figure 4

This analysis indicates that the best place for John, given his preferences and perceptions, is Job C.

This technique can be adapted to situations where there are multiple persons involved in the decision process, e. g. where three siblings are making a decision about the best way to care for an aging mother, or a husband and wife are choosing among multiple home purchase options. Each decision maker can complete a decision matrix and the results can be compared, debated and perhaps combined into one. (note that to work effectively, there should first be agreement about the criteria selected and the weights assigned to each criteria.)

Some Tips for Thinking Through Alternative Solutions

- Someone, somewhere has dealt with this issue or solved this problem before (or one very similar). You don't always have to reinvent the wheel. Sometimes "best practices" are best practices for a reason, they work. Search for those solutions and determine if one or more can be adapted to your situation. (search the internet, reference books, query experts, etc.)
- Have you faced a similar situation before? Analyze what worked and/or what didn't?
- Break down the issue or problem into segments, deal with the segments individually and combine the solutions.
- If there is one particularly difficult element to the issue, separate it out. Apply the most rigorous analysis to that element. Having solved it, the rest become easier. If you can't solve it, don't waste time on the other elements.
- Combine two or more alternatives to build a "better" one.
- Consider "inverting" the elements of a possible solution. Change the sequence of steps to see if that improves the solution.
- Examine the possibility of using a potentially negative consequence of an option to create a positive effect that cancels out the negative.
- Identify ways to test the option before committing.
- If cost is a constraint, evaluate ways to reduce the costs through: substitution, removing non-essentials, changing time schedules, changing sources, modifying specifications, etc.
- Check your conclusions against all available evidence.

Whether or not you use one or more *techniques*, each step of the process requires judgement. Good judgement comes from experience, education, logic and reason. Don't ignore judgment in favor of some formula. Apply good judgement to the process.

Sound reasoning is the <u>non-contradictory integration</u> of evidence, experience, values, knowledge and goals. Accurately assessing a situation involves *being fully aware* of circumstances and alternatives, *applying* knowledge, understanding and educated instincts to your analysis, *weighing* the implications for others and carefully *evaluating* the possible consequences. Think it through.

> "I think, therefore I am."
> Rene Descartes

10. <u>MAKE THE DECISION</u>

The time and effort you spend on various decisions will, and should, vary significantly. Two factors affect the appropriate time and effort involved. The expected consequences of the decision and the amount of time circumstances and pressures permit. Consciously match process time and effort to the impact the decision is likely to have. As soon as you have completed the analysis that the importance of the decision justifies, MAKE THE DECISION. Knowing *when* to make the decision is a critical element in making better decisions. You will almost never have all the information and time you would like. Reflect carefully on what you have and "pull the trigger."

Procrastination is the single greatest obstacle to effective decision making. Sometimes just getting started is the biggest hurtle. Start when you have enough time to complete the process. Allow time during the process to reflect, and to allow your sub-conscious to work. Avoid *Analysis Paralysis*. Don't get so bogged down in gathering and evaluating information that time and effort is wasted and/or time sensitive, viable and attractive alternatives are no longer available. Know when to start and when to quit.

Understand that not choosing is a choice. The opportunity may be missed or someone else may make the choice for you. Not deciding frequently leads to unsatisfactory outcomes. Take control. Make your own decisions.

> "More is lost by indecision than by wrong decision. Indecision is the thief of opportunity. It will steal you blind."
> Cicero

A major reason for procrastination is FEAR.

- *Fear of Failure* – Some people have difficulties making decisions because of the fear of making the wrong decision. If you have followed an effective process and thought it through carefully, you have done the best you can do. Some of your decisions will fail. That is inevitable because you are human, but a majority of your choices will be good ones. Don't let fear of making the wrong choice keep you from making a choice. When you make a mistake, learn from it and move on.
- *Fear of the Unknown* – Some have difficulties dealing with uncertainty. The future is uncertain. Focus on what you do know, gather information and rely on experts to fill the gaps. Keep moving toward your goals.
- *Fear of Change* - Some are uncomfortable with change. They fear that change may mean they lose control. Everything in life changes. Everything! Change is another word for evolution. *How* we evolve is our choice. *That* we evolve is not. Life is a process of continuous change. If we don't change, we lose touch

with reality. Learning changes (expands, alters) our minds. Change is how we grow. Your choices determine how you grow. Embrace change. Don't attempt to avoid it.

- *Fear of Rejection* – We hate to hear the word "no". We tend to take a "no" response to an idea, suggestion or choice very personally, interpreting it as a rejection of ourselves as well as the idea. Some go to great lengths to avoid hearing a "no", avoiding making decisions that might elicit a negative response. Listen carefully to a "no" response. Ask why. There may be valid reasons that you hadn't considered, and should take into account. Modifications may lead to a "yes". Don't let the possibility of a negative response deter you from making a decision.

- *Fear of Criticism* – Some become "frozen" because of concerns about meeting the expectations of others, especially if the others are persons close to them and whose approval and respect they covet. Do your homework. Consult persons you respect. Make your choice. Criticism hurts, but don't let the potential criticism of others keep you from doing what you have decided is the right thing to do.

In 1910, President Theodore Roosevelt included these remarks in a speech:

"It is not the critic who counts; nor the man who points out how the strong man stumbles, or where the doer of deeds could have done them better. The credit belongs to the man who is actually in the arena, whose face is marred by dust, sweat and blood; who strives valiantly; who errs, who comes up short again and again, because there is no effort without error and shortcoming; but he who actually strives to do the deeds; who knows great enthusiasms, the great devotions, who spends himself in a worthy cause; who at the best, knows in the end the triumph of high achievement and who at the worst, if he fails while daring greatly, knows that his place shall never be with those cold and timid souls who know neither victory or defeat."

A valid observation.

Focus on What is Important - There are typically only a few really important elements to a decision. Concentrate on the core issues. Ask yourself: what are the make or break elements of this decision? When having difficulty making a decision, ask yourself: "what's bothering me?" "What is it about this situation that is keeping me from promptly making the decision?" The answer will likely indicate where you should focus your attention.

11. IMPLEMENT

Once you have made the decision, develop a plan and implement it. Don't procrastinate. **The best decision you can ever conceive is meaningless unless implemented.** Identifying the best way to implement, will likely involve another set of decisions, decisions such as when and how. Apply what you have learned about decision making to the decisions about how to implement.

Develop an Action Plan. Write it down.

The value of a plan is in the planning process. It forces you to think. It is unlikely that things will go exactly as planned, but with a plan, you are much better prepared to respond and adapt to the unexpected. The purpose of a plan is not to lock you into a rigid set of steps, but to prepare you to adapt to developments and effectively achieve your objectives. It also establishes a standard, a measuring stick, against which to measure progress and determine completion.

Ask yourself these questions:

- What has to be done to make this decision effective?
- Who has to be informed, of what?
- Who has to do what?
- From whom do I need assistance?
- What are the important interim and final completion dates?
- What resources/tools are required?
- How will I track progress?
- How will I measure results?
- What are my contingency plans?

For some decisions, implementation is a simple one-step process. You decide and you do it. Others are more complex, involve multiple steps and require the involvement of others. Be sure the action plan includes: periodic checks to see if things are on track, follow up steps that are required, coordination with outside persons or organizations and a final review to see that all bases have been covered. Things do not always go as planned.

Demonstrate a bias for action. Don't just sit there. **Do something**.

> "I have been impressed with the urgency of doing. Knowing is not enough; we must apply. Being willing is not enough; we must do."
> Leonardo da Vinci

> "Perhaps the most valuable result of all education is the ability to make yourself do the thing you have to do when it ought to be done, whether you like it or not. It is the first lesson that ought to be learned and, however

early a person's training begins, it is probably the last lesson a person learns thoroughly."

Thomas Henry Huxley

12. <u>POST MORTEMS</u>

Don't succumb to the tendency to ignore or "forget" poor decisions and savor just the good ones. You learn to make decisions by making decisions. You will learn more about making decisions if you keep notes during the process and subsequently analyze both decisions that produced good results and those that did not turn out well. Ask yourself:

- What was the real reason I chose as I did?
- What are the real reasons this decision turned out well or poorly?
- Did I define the issue accurately?
- Did I consider all the realistic alternatives?
- What information should I have sought that I didn't?
- Was the information I used really relevant?
- Was there a way that I could have more realistically anticipated the consequences? What clues did I miss?
- What did I learn?
- Regardless of the results, what should I have done differently in the process?

Do not judge choices solely by results. The quality of the process counts. "Good" decisions can have poor consequences and "poor" decisions may turn out well. **The objective of the postmortem process is to learn things that will help you make better decisions in the future.**

Acknowledge your constructive decisions. Reflecting on the positives helps build confidence and self-esteem, which leads to better decision making. Ask: "what did I learn that I can apply in the future?" Analyze, don't rationalize, the dysfunctional ones. Ask: "what did I learn that I can apply in the future?"

Don't use the post mortem to beat yourself up for mistakes, but to improve your skills for making future decisions. You will never bat 100%, but over time making good choices will lead to better consequences and good decisions will lead to more good decisions.

Also bear in mind that it is not at all practical to review every decision. This analysis should be reserved for important decisions, those that have significant consequences.

> "Some of the best lessons we ever learn are learned from past mistakes. The error of the past is the wisdom and enabler of the future".
> Dale Turner

> "A man who has committed a mistake and doesn't correct it, is making another mistake."
> Confucius

Should you consciously apply each of these steps to every decision you make? Of course not, life is too short. The focus of this discourse is on improving the quality of critical, significant and important decisions. Through employing the process for those, you will come to intuitively apply the **principles** and the **mental discipline** to your mundane, routine decisions and inevitably improve the quality of those as well.

The dominant excuse for not employing an effective process in decision making is the *"I don't have time"* rationalization. There is a lot of truth to the old adage that "if you don't have time to do it right the first time, you will have to make time to do it over again". The key is to match the time and effort you invest in the decision to the importance of the issue, and the potential impact of the consequences. Make the time to give important decisions the attention and effort they warrant.

Time can have a major impact on the quality of decisions. We rarely have all the time we would like for considering important decisions. Procrastination almost always has negative consequences. Putting off decisions until there is little time for analysis and reflection often leads to poor choices and may mean that the best alternatives are no longer available.

While employing an effective process is very important, it is not the only determinant of the quality of decisions. **Of even greater importance is the wisdom we bring to the process.** Our knowledge, experience and mindsets have a significant impact on the effectiveness of our decisions

It's important to understand the interconnectivity of decisions. Decisions affect other decisions. The fundamental decisions we make about the really important elements of life: values, morals, goals, objectives, relationships, our worldviews, priorities and attitudes, all profoundly affect the other choices we make. Making effective decisions about these elements lead to better choices in all aspects of our lives.

The focus of this text is to promote an understanding of how important decisions are to developing fulfilling and meaningful lives, and to present and encourage a comprehensive, holistic and effective approach to decision making.

We are the product of our decisions. Every important decision we make is an opportunity to impact the quality of our lives.

PART VI. HOW MIGHT I BECOME MORE PRODUCTIVE?

MONEY MANAGEMENT

Effective money management requires a plan and some self-discipline. Sounds like work, right? It is, but like almost everything of value, worth the effort. It doesn't have to be hard work. It doesn't have to mean a life of self-sacrifice. It doesn't have to be super sophisticated or time consuming. It just means starting <u>now</u>, following some simple principles and sticking with it. The formula for financial freedom is really quite straight forward – spend less than you make and compound the savings over time. Unfortunately most people don't "get it". Only about 1% of Americans enjoy the benefits of financial freedom. The rest are consumed with making a living rather than making a life. Understand that financial security is determined, not by how much one makes, but by how much one keeps of what one makes.

There is nothing wrong with the American Dream of owning a home in a safe neighborhood, driving a reliable automobile, funding our children's education and retiring with enough money to live in reasonable comfort without fear of bill collectors ruining our day. Unfortunately, the American Dream is just a pipe dream for most. Research indicates that 50% of Americans have less than $25,000 in savings and 20% have nothing, nada, zilch. At the same time the average American owes more than $8,400 in credit card debt. Many live paycheck to paycheck sweating the stretching of the paycheck to cover the bills, pushing the panic button and pulling out the credit card to dig themselves a deeper hole, when the inevitable unexpected financial "emergency" comes up. Don't be one of them.

The following are some suggestions for developing a plan, avoiding the financial worries that hound so many, and for achieving financial security. I hope that you will not "excuse" yourselves out of financial security and pay the price. You don't have to.

Pay Yourself First - The foundation of financial security is to <u>pay yourself first</u>.

1. First, set up an emergency fund and build it to at least 2 to 3 months of expenses. Make payments into the account automatic, every payday. Don't tap the emergency fund for anything other than an "emergency". If you have to tap it for an emergency, replenish it.
2. Establish an objective. Resolve to spend no more than 75% to 80% of take-home pay. That target may be difficult at first, but start, and work to getting to that level over a targeted time period.
3. When the emergency account is funded, make the same payment into a retirement account for which your payments receive income tax advantages (IRA, 401K etc). (By paying yourself in a tax-deductible account before you pay income tax to Uncle Sam, it costs less to fund your saving. For example: If you are in the 15% tax bracket, it only costs you $.85 in "cash" to put $1.00 into a tax-deductible saving account, and you earn interest on $1.00 instead of $.85).
   a. Fund it modestly at first but increase the amount over time.
   b. Make the account one that receives beneficial tax treatment, e.g., an Individual Retirement Account (IRA), 401k pension plan, Self Employed Pension (SEP) etc.
   c. Make the payment to the account "Automatic" (have it deducted from your paycheck or set it

up as an automatic bill payment from your checking account).

From Where Does the Investment Money Come? - It can come from what you are spending for other "things". Track every dollar that you spend. Paying by check makes tracking easier. Avoid writing checks for chunks of cash. It makes tracking more difficult. Save receipts. Each month itemize and analyze your expenditures.

If you are living "paycheck to paycheck" and think that you have nothing "left to save", you have to find a way to reduce expenditures. Find your "Latte" Factor(s). (this term was coined by a financial advisor whose client told him his advice was unrealistic for her because she had to spend all of her paycheck just to pay her bills and had no money "left" to save. When they tracked her expenditures they found she was spending an average of $11.20 per day at Starbucks). By paying herself the over $3,000 per year she had been putting into Starbuck's coffers, she had a start on building long term financial security.

Most people living paycheck to paycheck wish they had more income. They search for and wish for a bigger paycheck. The problem is <u>not what we earn but what we spend.</u> The key is to control spending.

Everyone spends money that is not "necessary". Identify your unnecessary expenditures, and start using that money to fund your future.

One of the most common is "eating out". It is one of the most extravagant things we do regularly. Every time that we eat at a restaurant we are paying for:

Building rent
property taxes

repairs & maintenance to the building
the employees' wages & benefits
the employees' social security taxes.
Utilities
operating & office supplies
cost of the food
(often) franchise fees
the owner's profit

The cost of the food we consume in a restaurant is typically about 25% of what we pay. We can prepare the same food at home for a fraction (1/4 or less) of the cost. I'm not saying that we should never eat in a restaurant, but limiting the frequency to special and necessary occasions can save a lot of money that can be invested for greater benefits.

The key point is to find expenditures that are not necessities (expenditures for entertainment - streaming, subscriptions, tickets etc. are another lucrative source), and turn that cash into investments.

The Power of Compound Interest - Compound interest is the concept of earning interest on interest. By leaving earned interest in an investment account, you can earn interest on that interest during the next time period and every period thereafter. Albert Einstein is reported to have described compound interest as the most powerful force in the universe.

The impact can be amazing. An investment of $100 per month for 30 years (a total of $36,000), invested at an 8% return will have accumulated to $141,600 at the end of the 30 year period. An investment of $360 per month (a total of $172,800) with an annual return of 6% will accumulate to $1,000,000 in 40 years.

Time and compound interest are the investor's best friend. Start as early as possible, but start now, no matter what your age. Invest as much as you can to start, and continue to increase the amount over time. The total accumulated is dependent upon the period of time, the rate of return and the amount contributed. Of the three variables, time has the greatest impact. The longer the interest compounds, the bigger the nest egg.

Conversely, interest can be a major negative, if you are paying it instead of collecting it. It significantly increases the cost of anything purchased "on time".

Consistency Counts - A critical element of the plan is consistency. The time to start is now. Select a percentage of your gross income that you will invest. Pay yourself first. Increase the percentage of income whenever possible. If your income goes up (e. g. a raise), promptly add a significantly larger percentage of the increase to the base before you get used to spending the increase.

Where to invest Your Funds - There are lots of alternatives. You want a balance of safety and return on investment. Your choices should reflect your tolerance for risk, your specific time horizon (years until retirement) and your desire for growth. Select a balance that lets you sleep nights. The following reflect my opinions and prejudices. They are not the ultimate answers. Read and get advice. Professional advice can be expensive and of little value, so be careful about paying for it.

1. If you are fortunate enough to have an employer who matches all or part of your contributions to a retirement plan, (such as a 401k), contribute, at the very least, what the employer will match. That matching money is like a gift. It significantly increases your rate of return.

2. If safety is your overriding objective, federally insured savings accounts and Treasury Bills offer the safest choices, but offer minimal returns.

3. Annuities from reputable companies are usually safe, but are designed to make money for the provider, not so much for the purchaser. Returns are a little better than the above, but I suggest that you avoid them.

4. Bonds are generally considered safer than stocks, but their asset value can vary with changes in interest rates (over which you have no control) and the returns are usually not very attractive.

5. I have a preference for common stocks. Common stocks have grown at an average of 8% to 9% per year over the last fifty years. That is an average. There have been huge swings in some of those years. Even well considered stocks offer a range of risk, but in general offer the highest return to risk relationship.

   Unless you are prepared to invest a lot of time and effort studying investing and a lot of time and effort selecting and following stocks, do not attempt to purchase individual stocks.

6. Mutual Funds permit you to invest in a pool of stocks, which reduces your risks and puts your money in the hands of a professional money manager. There are some exceptions, but most fund managers have historically done little or no better than the overall market. The fees for their expertise are out of proportion to the results and eat into your returns. I suggest you not go there. Early in my experience with investing, I placed some money with one of the leading mutual funds. The market declined. In seven months the value of my mutual fund investment declined by 22%. I then received a letter from the mutual fund company informing me that their fee schedule was set up as a % of the asset value in the account, and since my account

was now in a lower bracket, they would henceforth be charging me a higher fee. They lost 22% of my money and as a result wanted me to pay them more. I said no thanks.

7. A relatively new investment tool, and one growing in popularity, is called an Exchange Traded Fund, or ETF. Warren Buffett, one of the greatest investors of all time, recommends ETFs as the instrument of choice for amateur investors. I agree. ETFs invest in a pool of stocks so they provide diversification and the fees are much lower than mutual funds. You can buy ETFs that mirror the market by investing equally in all companies in the Standard & Poors 500, or you can buy ETFs that invest in all companies in a particular sector of the market, such as pharmaceuticals, or technology. Sectors pass in and out of favor, so owning shares of two or three ETFs invested in different sectors, for which trends are positive, probably makes sense. Such a plan provides higher probability of growth than a general market ETF, but more diversification than you get with just one sector.

I suggest that you <u>not</u> use a stockbroker because of the fees involved. I pay $55 to either buy or sell a stock through a stockbroker. I pay $6 for the same transaction on TD AMERITRADE, an on-line trading platform that costs nothing to join and provides an abundance of online education. Schwab has a similar service.

Own a Home - Make owning your own home a priority. It not only makes economic sense, the intangibles, the feelings it enables, are worth the effort. Save for a down-payment and shop for low down payment mortgages (like an FHA loan) at a reputable lender.

When you pay rent, you are making the mortgage payment for the landlord, paying his property taxes, paying his insurance bill, paying the interest on his loan, and paying him a profit. Owning your own home is another opportunity to pay yourself first. The amount of your monthly mortgage payment applied to principle is increasing <u>your</u> equity, not some landlord's.

Increase the Frequency of Mortgage Payments — Most mortgages are set up for monthly payments. Each payment is applied first to interest. The remaining portion of the payment reduces the balance of the loan. With monthly payments you are paying interest on the unpaid balance for one month.

If you get paid twice monthly, it is usually easier to budget two equal payments. It also has the advantage of increasing the amount of each payment that is applied to reducing the loan principal and thus the amount of interest you pay over the life of the loan. If you make a payment on the 15th, equal to half the monthly payment due on the 30th, more of the payment on the 30th (and all subsequent periods) will go towards the principal. Your monthly cash outlay is the same. This simple change will not amount to a huge savings over the full term of a mortgage, but better the benefit go to you than in interest to the lender.

More significant savings can be realized by making non-required, principal only, payments during the life of the mortgage. Just be sure that if you make this kind of payment, you do not have a use for the funds that represents a higher return, e. g. don't make an extra payment on a 4% mortgage while carrying debt on a credit card on which you are paying 16%.

Before you make any kind of an early payment, be sure that you will receive the full benefit. Some lenders don't allow partial or early payments, some charge a fee for the option and some simply will not credit the early payment until the due date, thus negating any advantage to you. Shop for a lender that offers you prepayment options and be sure the language of the loan document permits you the benefits.

Debt - Avoid buying anything on "time" except a home and the first automobile. For anything else, pay cash. Never finance "toys" or entertainment. If you can't pay cash now, figure out how much you can save per week to fund the purchase, and defer the purchase until you have the money saved to pay cash. Pay bills with funds earned, not with money you hope to make in the future.

Credit Cards - Credit cards are convenient and sometimes useful. You should probably have two. But credit card interest is disastrous to financial health. For example: If you have $2,000 in credit card debt, and make only the minimum payment each month, it will take you eighteen years and $4,600 to pay off the $2,000, if you never charge another dime on the credit card. It is hugely more advantageous to put that extra $2,600 into an account to earn interest <u>for</u> you, than to give it to the credit card company.

The power of compound interest cited above can work against you as well. If your minimum payment on a credit card is not at least as much as the interest, the next month you are paying interest on last month's interest. It will snowball.

Don't put anything on a credit card that you do not have the ability and determination to pay off completely when the next bill arrives.

Buying a Car - Never buy a <u>new</u> car. The value of a new automobile drops significantly the moment you drive it away from the dealership. The loss of market value over time is a significant portion of the total cost of owning a car. Studies indicate that the total cost of owning a car, (loss of market value, insurance, repairs and maintenance, etc) is the lowest when the vehicle is purchased 18 to 30 months after it is new. A good rule of thumb is to buy one with less than 35,000 miles and sell it when it reaches 150,000 to 175,000 miles, before significant repairs are required. You can usually get more selling it yourself than trading it in to a dealer.

Finance the first purchase for as short a period as you can afford. Make the payments automatic. Have them deducted from your checking account. IMPORTANT! <u>When you have it paid off, continue to make the same payment – to yourself.</u> Set up a separate savings account, and continue to make the "car payment" into that account every month. You have been getting along without the car payment amount. Continue to do so. When it comes time to purchase the next car, those savings and what you receive from selling your current car can provide enough funds for you to pay cash for your next car. Consider the following example:

Assumptions:

- You purchase a 2 year old car with less than 30,000 miles for $18,000
- You pay $1,000 down and finance $17,000 for 36 months at 5.5% interest.
- Your payments are $513.33 per month. (over the 36 months, you pay $1,480 in interest for the car loan, thus the cost of the car was not $18,000 but $19,480).

- After you pay off the loan in 36 months, you put $500 per month into a savings account.
- After another 24 months, you have $500 X 24 = $12,000 in the savings account.
- You sell your 7 year old car with less than 130,000 miles for $8,000.

- You have (12,000 + 8,000) $20,000 to pay cash for the next car.

- You reduce your monthly "payments" to your car savings account to $300. (put the other $200 into your retirement account).
- At the end of 60 months you have $18,000 in the account. You sell your car for $7,000 and have $25,000 to pay cash for the next car.

You have a new (used) car every five years and never (after the first one) pay interest on a car loan again.

Again, make it automatic. Have the "payments" deducted from your checking account.

Never, ever lease a car. The automobile lease is an ingenious scheme to make money for dealers and financial institutions. By making lease payments, the lessee is paying the interest, depreciation, manufacturer's profit, and dealer profit without accumulating any equity. At the end of the lease period, you have nothing.

This is not the time or place for a full course in financial management, but only a few tips to help avoid the big traps and get moving in the right direction. I suggest that you read The Automatic Millionaire by David Bach and take Dave Ramsey's course in money management. It is offered all over the country, often in churches.

PLANNING

The primary reason for the failure of projects is the failure to adequately plan. Planning increases the odds that outcomes will be positive. Planning is not just for businesses. It is critical for personal productivity and for achieving desired results. The value of planning is not in the plan, but in the process.

Planning is a mental process of thinking through what is desired and how it will be achieved. Planning should start with objectives, with the end in mind. Visualize the desired results, examine the premises, anticipate obstacles and brainstorm how to overcome them. Plans are commitments to courses of action resulting from the planning process. If the project is at all complex, write down the plan. It forces you to think.

Planning is concerned with the future, but the objective is not to determine what should be done in the future but rather what should be done now to make positive things happen in the future. Planning is a learning process. Planning should become an attitude, a way of life.

If you want to accomplish something, develop and follow a plan.

GETTING THINGS DONE

Almost all of us feel like we have too much to do and not enough time to do it. We sometimes, if not constantly, feel overwhelmed by all that we have to do. A USA TODAY article reported that a Gallup Poll, conducted in 2018, indicated that 55% of Americans felt stressed. Some of us react to being overwhelmed by working harder and longer. That approach rarely works. It typically increases stress, because we miss important events and opportunities in our lives. What we really need is a systematic way to work more effectively, to get more done in less time. Being more productive at tasks we have to complete means we have more time for things we "want to do", and also reduces stress levels.

Improving effectiveness involves viewing tasks in a different way and systematically organizing one's work and one's life. I found a system, that helped me significantly, in a book titled *Getting Things Done,* by David Allen. I recommend it. Allen is a management consultant and educator who has made a career out of helping people be more productive.

I will attempt to synthesize the concepts, guidelines and process here, but please recognize the limitations of trying to convey the wisdom of an entire book in a few paragraphs. The approach I will outline includes modifications to the Allen system that I have made to fit my circumstances and style. I suggest that you read the book.

What You Need:

- An "In-Box" (or boxes if you work in multiple locations) – a physical container for all information relevant to tasks you need to complete.
- Multiple lists (either paper or electronic).
    - Task List, for short tasks.
    - Active Projects List.
    - Later Projects List.
    - "Waiting for" List.
    - Contacts List.
- A Project Plan for each Active Project
- A physical file folder for each Active Project.
- A physical file folder for each Later Project.
- A Calendar – paper or electronic
- A (physical, portable) Read & Review folder.
- Adequate file space, readily accessible and organized by category.

The Process

1. Gather/Capture everything that you need to get done, everything that requires that you take some action.
2. Put everything, temporarily, into your In-Box.
3. Create and label categories for every aspect of your life.
4. Create Lists:

a. Short Term Task List – this list is for the simple, one or two step jobs that need to be done and typically can be done in less than a day. – returning phone calls, answering emails, etc.

b. Active Projects List – for more complex jobs that are multi-step and will require deliberation and focus.

c. Later Project List – more complex, multi-step jobs, without due dates, that can be deferred, but that you don't want to lose track of, and want to review periodically to determine if they should be moved to the Active Projects List.

d. "Waiting For" List – for information that you need and have requested from some source, but that has not shown up yet.

e. Contacts List – Name, address, telephone numbers, email addresses of everyone to whom you may at some time want to reach out.

5. Set up a filing system by category & sub-category.

6. Process promptly everything in your inbox – decide what it is and what needs to be done.

7. Discard items that do not require action and are not useful for reference.

8. Record each task to be done on one of your lists. The benefit here is to get things off your mind without losing track of them. The objective is to free your mind to: process, develop plans, solve problems, make decisions, and create opportunities, not serve as a "warehouse" for all the things you have to do. If you attempt to keep track of all you have to do in your mind, those things keep "popping up", distracting you from what you could be accomplishing, and you will inevitably "forget" some of them. Both of those results reduce effectiveness and create stress.

9. Create a project file for each active and later project.

10. File projects by category.
11. Develop a Project Plan for each Active Project.
12. Create a "Reference" file for each category.
13. File relevant information in your project & category files.
14. Place Read & Review items in your R&R folder.
15. Add new items to your In-Box as they come up.

Some Guidelines

1. Collecting – Be sure you collect everything: urgent, not urgent; long, short; now, later; important, trivial; **Everything,** from all sources: conversations, letter, email, telephone, your mind. If there is not a hard copy, jot a note for your In-Box. Add everything that comes up to your In-Box immediately.

2. Categories – Think about the logical divisions in your life and set them up as categories. For major categories, create sub-categories. For example: I help owners and investors buy and sell commercial real estate. My "Work" category is set up as:

> Commercial Real Estate
> Current Listings
> Potential Listings
> Potential Buyers
> Prospecting
> Education
> Reference Information

One of my hobbies is photography. My "Photography" category is set up as:

> Photography
> Camera – Capabilities & Operation
> Techniques

Developing – Lightroom
Education
Printing
Field Trips
Reference Information

Other categories include: Family, Personal, Financial, Home Projects, Service, etc. etc. Create the categories important in your life.

3. Processing Items from Your In-Box
    a. Examine each item. Decide what it is and what action is appropriate.
    b. Add any that require action to one of your lists. If any of the tasks have due dates, note the due date with the title of the task.
    c. Add any that pertain to a project to the appropriate project file.
    d. Add reference material to the appropriate reference file.
    e. Place read & review material in your Read & Review folder.
    f. Discard all that do not require action or filing.
    g. Process your In-Box regularly, at least twice a day.
    h. Set regular times for processing your In-Box. If something interferes, reschedule.

4. Managing Your Short Term Task List.
    a. Schedule a daily start time and time duration for working on your short term list. If something interferes, reschedule
    b. Peruse your list for due dates to establish priorities.
    c. Take the appropriate action.

d. Physically check off each item as completed. It reinforces a feeling of progress.

5. Project Plans – Your Active Project List serves as a reminder of the projects requiring attention. For each active project, create a Project Plan that includes the following:

   a. The name of the project.

   b. Why you need to complete the project. It may be because your supervisor demands it or because your spouse would appreciate it. Knowing "why" helps you get focused and reinforces motivation.

   c. The **Desired Outcome** of the project. To determine how to get there, you have to know where you want to go. You can't determine what actions are appropriate until you know the outcome you want. Think through what you want the results to be. Defining results enables you to be more creative, more focused, and more effective.

   d. An indicator of the level of importance of the project

   e. The due date

   f. The information you need to complete the project.

   g. The **Next Action Required.** This is a critical element of the system. It turns a wish list into an actionable plan. It discourages procrastination. It closes the gap between the present and what you want the future to be. It defines the next thing to do to move the project toward completion. Reminders won't get you there. Only specific actions will. Identifying those actions provides the motivation and the energy to get the job done. Determine as many "next actions", in sequence, as possible but always identify at least one. Then do it.

A Project Plan outline is shown in Appendix B.

6. Managing Projects
    a. Schedule a time and duration of time each day to work on projects. If something interferes, reschedule.
    b. Based on the Desired Outcome, make a judgement about the project's level of importance.
    c. Check due dates and level of importance to establish priorities.
    d. Define and complete Next Actions Required.
    e. Start with the project with the highest priority. Complete as many of the Next Actions Required as you can with the information currently available. If you can't complete the project, always determine and note the Next Action Required.

7. Filing – Don't underestimate the value of developing and maintaining an accessible and functional filing system. The ability to quickly find what you need is critical to productivity. Don't stack it, file it.

8. Calendar – Keep three kinds of information on your calendar:
    a. Appointments
    b. Things you need to do on a specific day but not necessarily at a certain time.
    c. Information you need by a specific day to complete an active project on time.

Review and update your calendar early in the day or at the end of the day for the next day.

9. Waiting For – Your "Waiting For" list is to keep track of information you need that you have requested or ordered from some source. Review it daily to determine if you need to find another source or remind someone that they owe you a response.

10. Read & Review folder – as you process your In-Box you will inevitably find items you would like to read "when you have time". Keep a portable folder handy for these items. Read when you experience "wait time". Take the folder with you so you can read while waiting for a meeting to start or waiting for an appointment.

11. Reference Files – Put a label on, and place in your category or project reference files, items to which you may need to refer later, such as Instruction manuals, market or industry statistics, etc. You may also find it useful to have a "General Reference" file.

12. Later Projects – Ideas and information for projects to be tackled later should be captured and filed by project.

13. Review all your lists and projects at least once per week. Schedule a time for the review. Make sure that your lists include everything about which you need to take action, that you have defined Next Actions for all projects, and that everything that should be filed is filed.

14. Establish a designated place for everything, at work and at home.

15. Review/update your system and purge your files at least once per year.

In his book *THE ORGANIZED MIND*, Daniel Livitin recommends writing every task on a 3 X 5 card with a different colored card to separate the pack into categories. That is a powerful process. I find that it involves too many cards to shuffle. I have found it effective to keep a three ring binder on my desk with a master short term task list and a separate master project list in front, and project plans with task lists and progress notes behind tabs for each project. I keep one 3 X 5 card in my shirt pocket with a list of the tasks that I want to accomplish today. I prepare a new card daily.

Improving effectiveness is about managing actions. Think about what next actions will get you closer to achieving your goals and objectives. Make commitments to yourself. Renegotiate those commitments when necessary, but don't procrastinate. Focus on outcomes and the actions that will make the outcomes happen.

Read the Allen book, review these notes and create/modify a system that fits your circumstances, lifestyle and objectives. If you really get into the process, read Allen's sequel, titled *Ready for Anything*. It contains "52 Productivity Principles for Work & Life".

FOCUS

To achieve the best results we have to focus our attention. People who claim they can effectively multi-task are kidding themselves. What they are doing is constantly switching from one task to another, which is energy draining and very inefficient. The transition takes time and effort and prevents us from viewing subjects as whole. Studies have shown that it also increases stress. Our minds are not designed to hold two or more thoughts simultaneously or to handle two or more tasks simultaneously. The youth who attempts to do homework and watch television at the same time cannot grasp the best of either. If the TV program is more interesting than the homework, the homework will lose.

Focus also aids retention. Cognitive neuroscientist Sandra Bond Chapman, PhD, Director of the Center for BrainHealth at the University of Texas at Dallas, explains: "Chronic multitasking and constantly switching your attention from one thing to another disrupts the memory formation system. Allow yourself to focus on just one thing and go deep. This can change brain structure and brain function for the better."

Our minds are like gardens. If neglected they become overrun with weeds (mental clutter). If planted with the right seeds, cultivated and tended, they produce wonderful fruit.

> "Keep your mind off the things you don't want by keeping it on the things you do want."
> W. Clement Stone

Focused thinking clarifies objectives, concentrates energy and leads to higher levels of understanding. Thinking is accumulative. Good ideas and conclusions build on prior thoughts. Continuity is important. Superb athletes talk of "being in the zone", when everything comes together and works. Thinking functions the same way. We think best when we follow a "stream of thought", looking at a thought from different perspectives, weighing pros and cons and considering alternatives.

We can help focus our thinking by:

- Eliminating distractions.
- Scheduling time for focused thinking.
- Finding a quiet place for focused thinking.

- Setting targets, establishing a time/date by which you strive to have "thought through" a subject.
- Concentrating on the one task during the time designated.

SYNERGY & CONFLICT RESOLUTION

Getting things done often requires interacting with other people. Much of the stress in our lives is caused by these interactions becoming conflicts; in families, in the workplace, in organizations to which we belong, and in our communities.

Stephen Covey, in his book *THE 3rd ALTERNATIVE*, proposes a process for conflict resolution which he calls *Synergy*. The concept is to follow a process that leads to a solution that represents a third way, a "better way", rather than "my way" or "your way".

Most conflicts occur because the participants see things differently, have different worldviews, different backgrounds and have different ideas about solutions. Each participant often has definite opinions about the persons on "the other side" - unreasonable, foolish, heartless, etc. These perceptions get in the way of resolving the issue.

Fundamental to finding a better alternative is the *desire* to find one. A simplified overview of Covey's resolution process is as follows:

1. **Know yourself – recognize how you feel. If you are: angry, hurt, strongly disagree, acknowledge the fact.**

2. **Empathize – put yourself in the other's shoes**

3. **Reach out to the other – "you see things differently than i do. I need to hear you".**

4. **Listen – really listen**

5. **Ask the other if she/he is willing to work with you to find a better way. A way which you can both agree is better than the current solution proposed by either side.**

6. **Synergize**
   a. **Define what a better way would look like.**
   b. **Brainstorm new options together.**
   c. **Find a better way, a third alternative.**

Self Knowledge – First examine and understand your own assumptions, motives, prejudices and biases. Determine not just your side of the issue but also why you think the way you do. Question how accurate your notions are.

Empathy – Really try to see the other person as a unique individual, not representative of some group, not as a thing. Get past stereotypes. Honestly attempt to view the other with respect. Try to imagine why that person thinks the way she/he does.

Reach out to the other – Take the initiative. Make the first move. Engage with the other with a statement like: "You apparently see things differently than I do. I need to hear you. Tell me more."

Listen, really listen – Don't fake it. Be present. Empty your mind of everything else. Don't fall into the trap of framing your rebuttal while the other is stating his/her case. Don't get defensive. Reflect on what is stated. Ask questions in a non-threatening way. Think about "why". "To listen empathetically does not mean we agree with the other person's point of view. It does mean that we try to *see* that point of view." (Covey).

Appeal for collaboration – Sincerely invite the other to partner with you in seeking a solution different (better) than the ones considered to date. "Let's pool our ideas to see if we can come up with a 3rd Alternative, a win/win alternative." Point out what is at stake. Demonstrate that you are willing to expend the extra effort to find an acceptable solution and appeal for her/his help.

Synergize – First seek agreement about what a better solution would look like. Discuss and agree upon criteria. Be creative together. Consider radical possibilities. Seek new resources/relevant information. Brainstorm possible alternatives and test them against your criteria. Arrive at a Better Alternative.

Covey points out that Synergy is not the same as compromise. In a compromise, both parties "concede, sacrifice, or surrender some of their own interests in order to reach an arrangement". That is a "lose/lose situation. It is adding 2 + 2 to get 3.5. Synergy is adding 2 +2 to get 5. It is a win/win situation.

He also reminds us that "how we see things determines what we do, and what we do determines the results we get."

PART VII. WHAT'S IT ALL ABOUT?

SPIRITUALITY

At some point we wonder what it all means. Why am I here? Does life have meaning? What is the purpose of life? What am I supposed to do? Does God exist? Why is there suffering and evil? Why is there something rather than nothing? What happens to me when I die? Beliefs about these kinds of issues define one's spirituality. As used here, spirituality is not the same as religion. Addressing issues of spirituality is an attempt to understand the essence and meaning of life. There is value in pondering these issues, for they help shape how we live our lives.

I very strongly believe that one's spirituality/religion is very personal and a matter of individual choice. No one has the right to impose their beliefs upon another. That does not mean that it is wrong to share one's beliefs, but there is a huge difference between sharing and imposing.

Religion was the excuse for atrocities in the Crusades, the Spanish Inquisition, Catholic/Protestant conflicts in Ireland, Jihad and other "holy wars". The official records of the Spanish Inquisition indicate that the Inquisitors burned alive 300,000 human beings because the victims held religious beliefs different from those of the Inquisitors. Political leaders of Germany, labeled a Christian nation, annihilated six million Jewish persons. Spanish priests enslaved Native Americans in the Southwest to build churches to glorify God. The American Government and American religious denominations (churches) collaborated to wrench Native American children from their parents and incarcerate them in boarding schools to teach them the missionaries' version of religion.

I believe that doing another person bodily or psychological harm in the name of "God" is an abomination. Any religion that preaches hatred or disrespect for others because of their beliefs is illegitimate. A valid religion should align us with moral truths, motivate us to do good works and develop character. It should help us live with problems that don't have easy solutions, and realities that that don't have easy explanations. Its focus should be on principles that unite us, not doctrines that divide us.

The word "religion" comes from the Latin *religare*, which means "bind together". Persons with power in religion have far too often distorted that meaning, by emphasizing divisiveness rather than cohesiveness, by rejecting and condemning viewpoints different from their group's established norms and especially by rejecting and condemning all those who might hold contrary viewpoints.

I believe that one's spiritual/religious beliefs and practices should be the result of one's personal quest, never dictated by others. I also believe that one should be open minded about things spiritual, willing to learn and to allow spiritual growth to occur as one learns. I am convinced that no one religious tradition has a monopoly on the truth. I am a seeker, convinced that spiritual understanding becomes deeper and more revealing through study, reflection, sharing in discussion and, most of all, through practicing what we believe. The following statements represent some of what I currently believe, but would never insist that anyone else believe. They also represent standards to which I aspire, but do not always achieve.

- Spirituality is important. I work at understanding it, but acknowledge the limits of my understanding.

- I believe a respectful regard for all human beings and all living things, as well as living a moral and ethical life are the foundations of spirituality.
- I believe one of the basic goals of anyone's spiritual quest and any spirituality system should be to strive to find truth.
- I accept that, at the core, there will always be a great *mystery*. We will never find all the answers.
- I regard all life as sacred, interrelated and interdependent.
- I consider life precious. I attempt to remember to be grateful for the gift of life.
- I attempt to approach life with a genuine sense of awe. I find it helps to peer into the night sky and attempt to visualize the vastness of the universe, to savor the wonders of nature, and to gaze at a new baby and contemplate the miracle of birth, the creation of a new person.
- I continually seek truth, knowledge and wisdom about things spiritual.
- I want to be consistently compassionate and serving, but recognize that I often fall short.
- I strive to pursue worthy purposes and live a life that has meaning.

I share the above, not to convince the reader to agree with me, but to encourage her/him to think about what is really important.

I think there has to be an "Other", an ultimate power, that we have labeled "God". I cannot believe, as some contend, that persons are evolutionary accidents. I cannot believe it is an accident that the two cameras I have in my head, which I call eyes, can take two snapshots of the world I perceive and register it on my brain as a single image. I cannot believe that it is an accident that I can ingest flesh and plants that are converted into energy so I can work and play. I cannot believe that it is an accident that a sperm and egg can unite to form a new creature. I cannot believe that the wonders of my mind are an accident. Some power, which I am at a loss to understand, enables those and other miracles to happen.

Aldous Huxley very emphatically stated what he had concluded "What It's All About", in an essay titled *Seven Meditations*, written in 1943:

> "God is. That is the primordial fact. It is in order that we may discover this fact for ourselves, by direct experience, that we exist. The final end and purpose of every human being is the unitive knowledge of God's being."

In the same essay, he goes on to say:

> "Potentially (for in his normal condition he does not know who he is) man is much more than the personality he takes himself to be. He cannot achieve his wholeness unless and until he realizes his true nature, discovers and liberates the spirit within his soul and so unites himself with God."

Huxley, a prolific writer of nearly 50 books, numerous essays and works of poetry, was widely acknowledged as one of the preeminent intellectuals of the 20th century. Early in his career he was a self-described agnostic and regarded by many as an atheist. His initial works were severely critical of Christianity, as well as Eastern Religions. As he matured, he remarkably transformed to a Believer and a vocal advocate of the value of forming a personal relationship with God.

Science has revealed to us a lot about how the physical world works, about the vastness and wonders of space and the intricacies of the atom. That knowledge is a wonderful thing. It explains the "how" but not the "why". Science does not explain why we are here or the meaning of life. The latter issues are for our minds to explore,

Seek the truth. Understand that that you cannot hope to capture it all. Consciously make your spiritual decisions your own. Think about them, read about them, talk about them. Do not let someone else dictate what you believe. Be especially wary of those who claim to have all the answers. They don't. Beliefs are not irrelevant, because they influence our actions, but understand that true spirituality is not about what we believe, but about what we do, how we live.

One wise observation about spirituality is a summary written by Guy Murchie in his book, *The Seven Mysteries of Life*. It is not an explanation, but a description of our striving and the limits of our understanding.

DIVINITY

"Who or What runs the Universe?
Is there a plan behind the daisy, the hummingbird, the whale, the world?
Who conceived the eye back in the primeval darkness
Of early evolution?
Who designed the fish's air bladder in the ancient deep
As if foreseeing its future as a breathing lung
Upon the dry land.
And out of what beginning evolved the mind?
By any stretch could mind have been mindlessly created?
Does science have an answer
To the voice out of the Whirlwind Which asked Job
Who hath put wisdom in the inward parts?
Is the world really drifting along without pilot,

Steering itself automatically,
Running its own affairs at random?
Could the Universe, just conceivably,
Have created itself?

Surely there is Mystery in this Universe,
Not only somewhere and somewhen but
everywhere and everywhen
And far, far beyond the scope of man's feeble
Capacity to understand.
For man, puny mortal and finite,
As he is in this nether phase,
Is permitted to visualize neither an end to space
Nor space without end;
Nor can he even grasp a start or a finish of time,
Nor any sort of beginning that has no beginning,
Nor any end that has no end.

Hence the Mystery,
The abiding, pervasive, universal Unknowability
That many call by the name of God.
But what matters it what you call It?
It is abstruse, bewilderingly abstruse, and remains
so
Whether or no we accept that somehow by Its
agency
out of utter nothingness has risen
Everything in the Universe.

Its station plainly implies intelligence,
Indeed Intelligence so far beyond the human
As to justify the adjective "Divine".
And this seems to be relative.
If a human adult represents divinity to a baby or an
animal,
So must the animal be divine to a vegetable,
The vegetable to a mineral …
Likewise, as wrote Paul to the Corinthians,
"The foolishness of God is wiser than men,"

And there is presumably a hierarchy in Divinity
above
As well as below us--
Even as the doings and thoughts of humanity and
of Earth
Are but a negligible jot
In the eternal consciousness of God,
Even as the horizon of knowledge expands
outward from our planet
Accompanied by the inexorable horizon of Mystery
Which expands even faster and farther than
knowledge,
Leading man's consciousness
To new dimensions.

Thus doth Divinity
Embrace all the other six mysteries of life
Even though callow men comprehendeth it not,
Even though the Mystery remaineth
So far beyond earthly finitude
That no eye but God's own Eye
Hath the capacity to see
GOD.

PURPOSE

Selecting a purpose gives our lives a reason for being and a
focus. Our purpose should include a commitment to do
something meaningful to ourselves and in the service of
humankind. It starts with identifying the right path to walk, the
right way to live, and then selecting a purpose to which one is
willing to devote one's efforts. Ask: what does the world need
that I would feel good about providing? If one has a worthy
purpose, a plan and the persistence to pursue that purpose, it
makes life worth living.

"The purpose of life is not to be happy — but to matter, to be productive, to be useful, to have it make some difference that you lived at all".

Leo Rosten

Living meaningfully, also requires that we accept responsibility for our actions, recognizing we are co-creators through the choices we make. To find meaning, to live well, we must determine why we live, find a purpose, and then really live.

"They say there are two important days is your life: the day you were born and the day you find out why you were born.

Carl Townsend.

Having a purpose does not guarantee life will be easy. Learning to cope with adversity and suffering builds strength. What is important is, not the circumstances that befall us, but how we respond to those circumstances. The key question is not "is the path easy?", but, "is the path worthwhile?". We should periodically stop and assess our significant experiences, good and bad, and ask:

- "What did I learn from that?"
- "How can I use what I've learned to keep making progress?"

"We're here to add something, to construct, to preserve. To leave something good for those little ones who are going to come into our world. Let that motivation be so firmly established in your heart and mind that you can say, 'I will stand for this. I will live for this."

Bear Heart – Muskogee Creek, Native American.

In Viktor Frankl's book, *Man's Search for Meaning*, about the plight of Jews in the Nazi death camps of WW II, Frankl relates how he survived, but lost his wife and parents, and witnessed the deaths of many. From that experience, Frankl, a psychotherapist, developed a thesis that contends that others can control everything about a person except that person's attitude.

Frankl credited his survival, and that of others, to adhering to the principles of: choosing an undefeated attitude, committing to values and goals, fulfilling one's responsibilities, serving others, demonstrating courage, seeking peace and pursuing happiness in the face of adversity. Later he stressed these principles in his psychotherapy practice and espoused them in his writings.

> "Don't go after happiness; rather commit yourself to something bigger than yourself, and let happiness come chasing after you."
> Viktor Frankl

MEANING

How we perceive the purpose of our lives and what gives our lives meaning affects our decisions. Much has been written about the attempt to answer the question: "What is the meaning of life?" That question is too abstract. More useful questions are "What gives life meaning?", and "What can I do to make my life meaningful?" These are important questions. How we answer them determines how we focus our lives, how we spend our time and energy and ultimately the value, the worth of our lives.

> "To be what we are and to become what we are capable of becoming is the only end of life."
> Robert Louis Stevenson.

We are programmed to want our lives to have meaning. Our lives will be meaningful if we accept the responsibility for making them so, and if we work at it. "Working at it" can be outlined as a process:

- Develop a vision of the person you would like to be, the kind of person you would be proud to be. Write down that vision.
- Think through what you would need to do to make that vision a reality. Write down those things.
- Make decisions. Take action.
- Reflect on your experiences. To what extent did you guess right? What did you learn? Did your decision help you become, or detract from your becoming, the person you want to be?
- Weigh and apply what you learned as you make your next decision.
- Repeat the previous three steps.

Meeting your standards should be challenging. You will never achieve the ideal, but your life will be more meaningful, interesting and fun for having employed the process.

> "The meaning of life is not to be found in having lots of money, fame, prestige or stuff. It is to be found in living a worthy quest for positive achievement. Make a difference in the lives of other people, make a difference for good. Create new relationships, new feelings, new forms of goodness in the world, by what you do and who you are. You will find in that process a sense of fulfillment that we so often seek in all the wrong places."
>
> Tom Morris

> "Beyond work and love, I would add two other ingredients that give meaning to life. First, to fulfill

whatever talents we are born with. Second, we should try to leave the world a better place than when we entered it."

Michio Kaku

Those of us who are parents should recognize that how effectively we teach our children principles and values has a significant impact on the success of our efforts to make the world a better place because we lived, for we can claim a little credit for the good they do in the world.

The Search for Meaning - Many of us live lives, not of quiet desperation, as Thoreau described, but of a clanging desperation. We are stressed daily by stories of man's inhumanity to man and evidence of a global environmental crisis that raises legitimate questions about the ability of our planet to long sustain life as we know it. Many have become disillusioned by our modern culture's pervasive emphasis on materialism. We acquire more things, but owning more things never seems to be *enough*. Pressing schedules make it seem as if there is never enough time.

It is important to understand that everything one says and does has consequences.

> "No teaching for the path of action could be more fundamental or primary than the teachings of love and respect – for oneself, for one's world and for the Great Spirit, which is all life in all things. The aspirant can perform no greater service for his world than to be mindful that his acts, even his thoughts and speech, become a part of the condition of the world."
> Rolling Thunder – Cherokee

Many are searching. Some search for answers in all the wrong places. Some would like answers but won't make the effort to search. To some, despite feelings of emptiness and desperation, the idea of searching never occurs.

There is nothing wrong with being happy, but personal wholeness, not happiness should be our focus. Strive to live a life of purpose, righteousness and virtue. Happiness will happen.

Consciously or unconsciously, we wonder about the meaning of it all.

> "Life has been given to us not so that we can spend it in idle enjoyment. No, life is a struggle and a series of battles: the struggle of good with evil, of fairness with injustice, of freedom with oppression, of true love with desires of the flesh. But we need to remember this not merely in order to criticize contemporary life, but so as to establish a better life for all. We need to believe that life has to be better than it is at present, and to live our lives in such a way as to make it better."
> Leo Tolstoy

The search for meaning should be based on understanding that everything is interdependent, that humans must be aware that everything they do impacts other beings, and that one's purpose is to help take care of others.

> "Challenges are what make life interesting and overcoming them is what makes life meaningful."
> Joshua J. Marine

Mother Teresa, the nun and missionary who dedicated her life to alleviating the suffering of the "poorest of the poor", who was awarded the Nobel Peace Prize and canonized as a Saint, had these things to say about living a life of love and meaning:

"People are often unreasonable, illogical and self-centered:

Forgive them anyway.

If you are kind, people may accuse you of selfish, ulterior motives.

Be kind anyway.

If you are successful, you will win some false friends and some true enemies.

Succeed anyway.

If you are honest and frank, people may cheat you.

Be honest and frank anyway.

What you spend time building, someone may destroy overnight.

Build anyway.

If you find serenity and happiness, there may be jealousy.

Be happy anyway.

The good you do today, people will often forget tomorrow.

Do good anyway.

Give the world the best you have, and it may never be enough.

Give your best anyway.

You see, in the final analysis, it is between you and God. It was never between you and them anyway."

MOTHER TERESA

Great advice from a wise lady who had the integrity to practice what she preached. Go thou and do likewise.

Meaning is to be found by living the "right" way. One has many "roads" from which to choose, but only one is the "right road". This means living one's life consistent with the principles and values of:

- reverence for the Sacred
- reverence for nature
- truth
- integrity
- honor
- balance & harmony
- compassion
- generosity
- courage
- respect for the rights and ideas of others
- respect for elders
- rearing children of good character
- personal responsibility
- patience
- perseverance.

Finding meaning involves selecting a set of values and principles, living a life consistent with those values and principles, selecting a worthy purpose and pursuing that purpose to the best of one's ability.

One way to find meaning is by making a difference in the lives of others.

> "Learn to light a candle in the darkest moments of someone's life. Be the light that helps others see; it is what gives life its deepest significance."
> Roy T. Bennett

One of my high school friends emailed this to me. I don't know the name of the author. It expresses some significant truths. I thought it worth sharing.

THE TRAIN OF LIFE

"At birth we boarded the train and met our parents. We believed they would always travel by our side

However, at some station our parents will step down from the train, leaving us to journey alone.

As time goes by, others board the train and they become significant, e.g. our siblings, friends, and even the love of our life and our children.

Over time, many will step down and leave a permanent vacuum. Others will go so unnoticed that we won't realize they have vacated their seats.

The train ride will be full of joy, sorrow, fantasy, expectation, hellos and goodbyes.

A successful journey comes from having a good relationship with all passengers, requiring that we give the best of ourselves.

The mystery, for everyone on the train, is not knowing at what station we ourselves will step down. So we must live in the best way we know how; loving, sharing, forgiving and offering the best of who we are.

It is important that we do this, because when it is our turn to step down and leave our seat empty, we should leave behind beautiful memories for those who continue the journey. The train will go on.

I wish you a joyful journey on the train of life. Reap lots of success and give lots of love.

I thank you for being one of the passengers on my train.

People will forget what you did. People will forget what you said. But people will never forget how you made them feel."

WISDOM

Wisdom is not about developing a specific proficiency or skill. It is about learning how to live. Achieving wisdom involves developing the ability to understand the real meaning of the ordinary and extraordinary things that happen in one's life. The acquisition and demonstration of wisdom is worthy of being one of life's highest aspirations. Seeking wisdom is a quest. The prime motivation for seeking wisdom is to develop the ability to determine the "right" way to live one's life, to consistently make effective decisions.

Wisdom involves the accumulation of knowledge and, more importantly, the understanding of how to apply that knowledge. Learning is an essential and lifelong pursuit. Accept challenges. Explore the unfamiliar. Practice healthy skepticism, ask questions. Questions lead to truth. Our goal should be to learn enough truth to have wisdom, to apply the right principles at the right time.

Many subscribe to the wisdom of the Buddha. The Buddha taught that wisdom is based upon:

- The Right View – seeing life as it really is, not as it appears or as you would like it to be.
- The Right Intentions – dealing with others with understanding and compassion.
- The Right Action – do no harm.

His teachings include Four Noble Truths, the application of which provide a prescription for healing, and for problem solving:

- Diagnose the problem.
- Identify the underlying causes.
- Determine the prognosis.
- Prescribe a course of treatment.

He taught that the causes of many problems can be traced to "The Three Poisons":

- Ignorance
- Desire
- Aversion

Hope is expressed in his contention that:

> "Every sentient being has the potential to improve and become enlightened."

Develop Wisdom - There are multiple, complex and interrelated elements to the development of wisdom:

- Spirituality is at the core of wisdom.
- Self-knowledge is fundamental. To see the world clearly, one must first understand oneself.
- Understanding, and applying, the right <u>principles</u> and <u>values</u> to all decisions are basics.
- Wisdom is acquired through experience, but experience does not automatically generate wisdom. It is the ability to reflect upon and learn from experiences that confers wisdom.
- Awareness and mindfulness are important to effective understanding and reflection.
- Receptivity to new ways of thinking and ordering facts and knowledge enhances wisdom.

- The ability to find balance and harmony between apparently conflicting objectives and perspectives demonstrates wisdom.
- Compassion, focusing on the "common good" rather than self-interest indicates wisdom.

Wisdom develops out of intellectual virtues, but is basically knowing how to behave and how to live in the absence of perfect knowledge.

Experiences contribute to wisdom. Life offers us wisdom, often in ways we do not initially understand or choose. Observation, awareness and listening are essential skills for developing knowledge. Integrity, personal character and good judgement are essential for applying that knowledge effectively. The fruits of wisdom are the calmness and peace of mind which come from self-control.

I mentioned earlier that not all of the material in this text is original. I "borrowed" this lighter note about the difference between knowledge and wisdom from a letter to the editor in *READER'S DIGEST*:

> "Knowledge is knowing that a tomato is a fruit.
> Wisdom is knowing not to put it in a fruit salad."

Wisdom must be tempered with compassion. To see things clearly requires viewing life through the "eye of the heart". The application of real wisdom requires the balancing of head and heart.

LOVE

The essence of a life of meaning is Love. Identifying what we love, paying attention to what we love, doing what we love, sharing what we love, these are factors that make life worth living. What we choose to love motivates us, moves us forward, shapes our lives, satisfies our longings. Love keeps us awake and alive.

> "and now these three remain: faith hope and love. But the greatest of these is love."
> 1 Corinthians 13:13

When we know what we love, we achieve a clarity of purpose and the capacity to act on what we believe. What we love we pay attention to:

> "Attention is the tangible measure of love. Whatever receives our time and attention becomes the center of gravity, the focus of our life. This is what we do with what we love: we allow it to become our center."
> Wayne Muller

What we choose to love is, of course, critical. We should love family, friends, ourselves, truth, integrity, beauty, giving and life. We should love what brings us and others benefit, not what does us harm.

How we love is equally important. Real love is unconditional. If our love is dependent upon another behaving a certain way or doing a certain thing, it is about loving ourselves, not the other person. Being real and caring, being there for someone, demonstrating kindness, these are the elements of love.

No matter our state of well-being, no matter how dire our circumstances, we all have the capacity to love. Exercising that capacity enriches our lives as well as the lives of those who are the recipients.

Ideally, we should love everyone, even those hard to love, or even like. That is extremely difficult. If we can't bring ourselves to love the rascals of the world, we should at least treat them as though we love them. We should also abandon any expectation that our acts of love will be reciprocated. It's not likely to happen. We should not make our love conditional.

A large part of "what it's all about" is trying to figure out how we can best live our lives within the inclusive context of our relationships with other humans and with the sacred, understanding that we are all interdependent and all in this together, striving to see the world more clearly, to see truth and reality.

PART VIII. THINK ABOUT IT!

CHOOSE TO THINK.

> "Just think. Just be quiet and think. It will make all the
> difference in the world."
>
> Mr. Rogers

People who live meaningful, effective and fulfilling lives think differently than those who don't. To accomplish anything, you have to take action, and the success of the action depends on the thoughts that initiated it. All that one achieves or fails to achieve is the direct result of one's thoughts.

Think about who you are. Think about who you want to be. Think about what you love. Think about what is sacred. Think about what is true. Think about what you want to learn. Think about your values and principles. Think about the fact that you will die and that this day is a gift. Think about what is important. Think about what is priceless. Think about how you wish to live your life.

Be a "critical" (not negative, but questioning) thinker. Ask: What evidence, experience, authority supports this statement, contention, theory? Is the evidence verifiable and complete? Are the premises valid? Are my intentions honorable, and right for all concerned?

Effective thinking is seeking the whole picture, looking for relationships, looking for patterns rather than pieces. To make effective decisions about how to live, it is critical to develop the ability to reason accurately and independently, rather than accepting answers based upon authority or tradition.

A collection of ancient Buddhist scriptures contains the following wisdom:

"Mind is the forerunner of all actions. All deeds are led by mind, created by mind. If one acts or speaks with a corrupt mind, suffering follows, as the wheel follows the hoof of an ox pulling a cart.

Mind is the forerunner of all actions. All deeds are led by mind, created by mind. If one speaks or acts with a serene mind, happiness follows, as surely as one's shadow."

We become what we think. To get control of our lives, we have to think, and control what we think.

"Self-control is strength; Right thought is mastery;
Calmness is power. Say unto your heart, peace be still."
James Allen

Clear thinking involves effectively gathering, accessing and integrating the multiple messages coming at us from the reality around us and within us. The characteristic that makes us uniquely human is the ability of our minds to examine their own processes, to think about thinking. We can, and should, mentally examine: How did I reach that conclusion? Was my conclusion influenced by my prejudices? Is my conclusion logical or does it reflect the way I want things to be? What are my goals and objectives? Will this decision enable or impede my goals? What kind of person do I want to be? Are my actions consistent with who I want to be?

Thinking is, of course, only the first step. The right thoughts are critical for they drive action, but what really matters is what we do. The objective is to produce the right results. The quality of results is almost always determined by the strength and quality of the thinking and the effort expended in achieving them.

"The Right Thought, plus the Right People, in the Right Environment at the Right Time for the Right Reason = the Right Result.

John C. Maxwell.

Words are powerful. Think before you speak. Empower the three gatekeepers of the Buddha's advice about speaking:

Is what I am about to say true?
Is what I am about to say necessary?
Will what I am about to say do no harm?

Thinking clearly takes commitment, effort and practice, but the benefits are well worth the effort. Our ability to think, and to think about thinking, is a tremendous gift. We use it or lose it.

Think About Your Current Reality.

- Am I a good mother/father?
- Am I a good daughter/son?
- Am I a good brother/sister?
- Am I a good spouse?
- Am I a good friend?
- Am I a good citizen?
- Do I always act morally, ethically?
- Am I living up to my potential? Could I be a better person?

If you are dissatisfied with the answers to any of these queries, think about how you might change your thoughts and behavior to align with who you want to be.

Think About Outcomes.

Determine what you really want and then about how to get there.

- How might my life be better if I change my priorities?

- How might my life be better if I change how I spend my time?
- How might my life be better if I develop _____ (a certain skill or ability)?
- How might my life be better if I treated _____ (someone) differently?
- How might my life be better if I learned _____?
- How might my life be better if I gave up _____?

RECOGNIZE THE IMPORTANCE OF DECISION MAKING

Decision making is the most important thing we do. When considering important choices, ask yourself: "does this choice reflect who I want to be?" We create ourselves through the decisions we make. Every choice we make is a decision, not only about what to do, but a decision about **Who We Are**.

Making better decisions requires both intention and attention. Effective decision making starts with awareness. Be aware that a decision is required and give the decision the attention it deserves. Decision making is a critical life skill, a skill that can never be perfected, but can be developed and significantly improved. We can make better decisions, if we want to do so enough to work at it. The meaning of our lives, our achievements, our happiness and our self-satisfaction all depend largely upon the choices we make. Recognize that this is so, and treat decision making accordingly.

It's your life. You are the one who should, whenever possible, make the decisions that affect it. Don't abdicate choices that should be yours, and always take responsibility for your decisions. Be sensitive to the significance of your decisions and develop the self-discipline to invest in each decision the effort it warrants. We take constructive ownership of our lives through the choices we make.

CHOOSE TO MAKE YOUR LIFE MEANINGFUL

Seek wisdom and do the right thing. Wisdom is about more than thinking. It is choosing to live wisely, aligning actions with valid principles.

> "Wisdom and right action are the same thing."
> Marcus Aurelius

Life is an endless quest, a search for wisdom and for experiences that enlighten. Finding meaning and purpose takes effort, introspection and wise choices about principles and values. It means being open to direction from a Higher Intelligence, searching inside for the real you. It involves deciding what kind of person one chooses to be and what kind of life one wants to live.

> "The value of life lies not in the length of days, but in the use we make of them; a man may live long yet live very little."
> Michel Eyquem de Montaigne

In the end, meaning is very personal. We each have a responsibility to determine a purpose for our lives that has significance for us. At least a part of that task is to develop ourselves into the most wise, moral, strong and loving persons we can be and to live in peace with a clear conscience. At the same time, we must understand that a "good" life is a process, not a state of being. We cannot be perfect.

> "We are visitors on this planet. We are here for ninety, a hundred years at the very most. During that time we must try to do something good, something useful with our lives. Try to be at peace with yourself and help

185

others share that peace. If you contribute to other people's happiness, you will find the true goal, the meaning of life."

The Dalai Lama

SEEK WISDOM

Everyone has something to offer. One should focus, not on what one can get or accumulate, but on what one can be and what one can give. The beginning of wisdom is determining what that should be, who you are and how you want to live. With wisdom comes an understanding of, and appreciation of, meaning.

The essence of wisdom is to understand that, despite our differences, humans are much more alike than different. We all live and we all die. We all hurt. We all laugh. We all cry. We all have problems. We all suffer losses. We all grieve. We all want to be loved. We all want to be respected. We all want to be treated fairly. We are all related. We are all the same. We are all in this together.

LET YOUR LIFE SPEAK

The real you is not revealed by what you believe or what you profess, but by what you do. Let the way you live your life demonstrate who you are. Doing good enables us to be good and to feel good.

Commit to truth.

Practice Integrity.

Live ethically and morally.

Serve others.

Search for understanding and wisdom.

Keep first things first.

Treat people with kindness and compassion.

Exert control of two things over which you have control, your attitude and your effort.

Support justice & fairness for all.

Forget about comparisons with and competition with others. Focus on being better than you used to be. Be dependable in times of challenge, straight in times of temptation and truthful always.

CHOOSE TO LIVE FULLY

Henry David Thoreau wrote that he wanted "to front only the essential facts of life, and see if I could learn what it had to teach, and not, when I came to die, to discover that I had not lived."

He chose to live. So should we. The world is a wonderful and mysterious place. It offers more possibilities than we can ever conceive. Try some of them.

Make a decision to make better decisions. Making better decisions will improve the quality of your life. One of the most important, fundamental, decisions we can make is to decide to live our lives, not just take up time and space, but really live.

Imagine you only have ten hours to live. What would you do?

Imagine you only have ten days to live. What would you do?

Imagine you only have ten months to live. What would you do?

Contemplate your answers to these questions. What would you do differently if you knew the exact amount of life you had left? How would you realign/refocus your life? Assuming that you would do something differently, why should not knowing the duration of your life keep you from starting that redesign now, from changing your focus now?

> "None of us know how much time we have to live, but we know it is finite. However long or short it is, we should live it to maximize: the joy of family and friends, service to others, and making the most of our potential. It's only when we truly know and understand that we have a limited time on earth – and that we have no way of knowing when our time is up – that we will begin to live each day to the fullest, as if it was the only one we had."
>
> Elizabeth Kübler-Ross

Develop a bias for action. Live life, don't just let it happen. DO SOMETHING to:

- Ease the burdens of others.
- Help others grow and realize their potential.
- Demonstrate kindness.
- Mold your character to align with valid principles.
- Learn, grow and realize your personal potential.
- Make something beautiful.
- Teach someone something useful.
- Promote social fairness and justice.
- Improve relationships between people.
- Preserve the wonder and beauty of nature.

It is in doing these things that we find meaning.

One of my favorite observations about life was written by George Bernard Shaw:

> **"Life is no brief candle to me. It is a sort of splendid torch which I have got a hold of for the moment, and**

I want to make it burn as brightly as possible before handing it on to future generations. I want to be thoroughly used up when I die, for the harder I work, the more I live. I rejoice in life for its own sake. This is the true joy of life: being used for a purpose recognized by yourself as a worthy one, being thoroughly worn out before being thrown on the scrap heap, being a force of nature instead of a selfish little clod of ailments and grievances complaining that the world will not devote itself to making you happy."

Every day, do something to make you a better you. Every day, learn something new. Every day, demonstrate compassion for someone. Regularly ask yourself, am I becoming the person I want to be?

Carpe diem. Life is precious! CHOOSE TO LIVE IT FULLY. This is not a rehearsal.

FRAMING WORKSHEET
Why is a Decision Required? What are the Root Causes of the Issue?
What is the Real Issue?

How Important is the Issue?	Comments
1 Paramount	
2 Significant	
3 Material	
4 Mundane	

What Are the Real Needs?

What Are My Objectives?
Primary:
Secondary:

What Are the Real Constraints?

What Are My Relevant Personal Preferences?

By When Should the Decision Be Made?
Required Date _____
Target Date _____

Comments

PROJECT PLAN WORKSHEET		
Project Title:		
Why is the Project required?		
The Desired Outcome		
How Important is the Project?	**Comments**	
☐ 1 Paramount		
☐ 2 Significant		
☐ 3 Material		
☐ 4 Mundane		
Information Needed to Complete the Project:		
Major Actions Required:		
1		
2		
3		
4		
5		
6		
7		
8		
9		
10		
11		
12		
By When Should the Project Be Completed?		
Required Date		
Target Date		
Comments		

POINTS TO PONDER

SOME THOUGHTS ABOUT HOW TO LIVE A MEANINGFUL LIFE

BIBLIOGRAPHY

Allen, David. *Getting Things Done: The Art of Stress-Free Productivity.* New York, NY. Penguin Books. 2003.

---------------- *Ready for Anything: 52 Productivity Principles for Work & Life.* New York, NY. Penguin Books. 2003.

Allen, James. *As a Man Thinketh.* White Plains, NY. Peter Pauper Press, Inc.

Bass, Diana Butler. *Grounded: Finding God in the World of Spiritual Revolution.* New York, NY. Harper Collins Publishers. 2017.

Baumeister, Roy F. and John Tierney. *Willpower: Rediscovering the Greatest Human Strength.* New York, NY. Penguin Group. 2011.

Bevelin, Peter. *Seeking Wisdom: From Darwin to Munger.* Malmo, Sweden. Post Scriptum, AB. 2003.

Bill, J. Brent. *Beauty, Truth, Life, and Love: Four Essentials for the Abundant Life.* Brewster, MA. Paraclete Press. 2019.

Branden, Nathaniel, Ph.D. *Taking Responsibility: Self Reliance and the Accountable Life.* New York, NY. Simon & Schuster. 1996.

--------- *The Art of Living Consciously: The Power of Awareness to Transform Everyday Life.* New York, NY. Simon & Schuster, 1997.

Brooks, David. *The Road to Character*. New York, NY. Random House. 2015.

Covey, Stephen R. *The 7 Habits of Highly Effective People*. New York, NY. Simon & Schuster. 1989.

--------- *First Things First*. New York, NY. Simon & Schuster. 1994.

--------- *The 8th Habit: From Effectiveness to Greatness*. New York, NY. Simon & Schuster. 2004.

--------- *The 3rd Alternative: Solving Life's Most Difficult Problems*. New York, NY. Simon & Schuster. 2011.

Covey, Stephen M. R. & Rebecca Merrill. *The Speed of Trust*. New York, NY. Simon & Schuster. 2006.

Dalio, Ray. *Principles: Life and Work*. New York, NY. Simon & Schuster. 2017.

Deloria, Vine Jr. *God is Red: A Native View of Religion*. Golden, CO. Fulcrum Publishing. 1994.

Diamandis, Peter M. and Stephen Kotler. *Abundance: The Future is Better than You Think*. New York, NY. Free Press. 2012.

Dickson, Douglas N., Ed. *Using Logical Techniques for Better Decisions*. New York, NY. John Wiley & Sons, Inc. 1983.

Divine, Mark. *Unbeatable Mind*. Mark Divine, 2015.

Frankl, Viktor E. *Man's Search for Meaning*. Boston, Ma. Beacon Press. 1959.

Garrett, Michael. *Walking on the Wind: Cherokee Teachings for Harmony and Balance*. Rochester, VT. Bear & Company, Publishers. 1998.

Gelb, Michael J. *How to Think like Leonardo da Vinci: Seven Steps to Genius Every Day.* New York, NY. Delacorte Press. 1998.

Goodenough, Ursula. *The Sacred Depths of Nature.* New York, NY. Oxford University Press. 1998.

Green, Alexander. *Beyond Wealth: the road map to a rich life.* Hoboken, NJ. John Wiley & Sons, Inc. 2011.

Hammond, John S., Ralph L. Keeney, Howard Raiffa. *A Practical Guide to Making Better Decisions.* Boston, MA. Harvard Business School Press. 1999.

Hahn, Thich Nhat. *The Miracle of Mindfulness: A Manual on Meditation.* Boston, MA. Beacon Press. 1975.

Holiday, Ryan. *Stillness is the Key: An Ancient Strategy for Modern Life.* London, Great Britain. Profile Books Ltd. 2019.

Huxley, Aldous. Edited by Jacqueline Hazard Bridgeman. *Huxley and God, Essays.* New York, NY. HarperCollins Publishers. 1992.

Johnson, Charles. *Grand: A Grandparent's Wisdom for a Happy Life.* Toronto, Ontario. Hanover Square Press. 2020.

Johnson, Richard P., PhD. *The 12 Keys to Spiritual Vitality.* Ligouri, MO. Ligouri Publications. 1998.

Johnson, Spencer, MD. *Yes or No: A Guide to Better Decisions.* New York, NY. Harper Collins Publishers, Inc. 1992.

Keyes, Ken Jr. *Taming Your Mind: A Guide to Sound Decisions.* Coos Bay, OR. Love Line Books. 1975.

Kubler – Ross, Elisabeth, & David Kessler. *Life Lessons.* New York, NY. Touchstone. 2002.

Levitin, Daniel J. *The Organized Mind: Thinking Straight in the Age of Information Overload.* New York, NY. Dutton. 2014.

Lindner, Ken. *Crunch Time: 8 Steps to Making the Right Life Decisions at the Right Time.* New York, NY. Penguin Books. 2005.

Mandino, Og. *A Better Way to Live.* New York, NY. Bantam Books. 1990.

Maxwell, John C. *Thinking for a Change: 11 Ways Highly Successful People Approach Life and Work.* New York, NY. Center Street, Hachette Book Group. 2003.

McGervey, John D. *Probabilities in Everyday Life.* New York, NY. Ballantine Books. 1989.

Minirth, Frank B. MD., Paul D. Meier, MD. *Happiness is a Choice.* Grand Rapids MI. Baker Book House. 1978.

Muller, Wayne. *How Then Shall We Live?* New York, NY. Bantam Books. 1996.

Murchie, Guy. *The Seven Mysteries of Life: An Exploration in Science and Philosophy*. Boston, MA. Houghton Mifflin Company. 1978.

Nerburn, Kent. *Voices in the Stones: Life Lessons from the Native Way.* Novato, CA. New World Library. 2016.

----------------- *Simple Truths: Gentle Guidance on the Big Issues in Life.* New York, NY. MJF Books. 1996.

Rahula, Walpola. *What the Buddha Taught.* New York, NY. Grove Weidenfeld. 1959.

Rath, Tom. *Life's Great Question: Discover How You Contribute to the World.* Jackson, TN. Silicon Guild Books. 2020.

Rinpoche, Yongey Mingyur, Eric Swanson. *Joyful Wisdom: Embracing Change and Finding Freedom.* New York, NY. Harmony Books. 2009.

Rogers, Carl R. *On Becoming a Person.* Boston, MA. Houghton Mifflin Company. Sentry Edition. 1961.

Rohr, Richard. *Falling Upward: A Spirituality for the Two Halves of Life.* San Francisco, CA. Jossey-Bass. 2011.

Schultz, Ron. *Unconventional Wisdom.* New York, NY. Harper Collins Publishers, Inc. 1994.

Shinabarger, Jeff. *Yes or No: How Your Everyday Decisions Will Forever Shape Your Life.* Colorado Springs, CO. David C. Cook. 2014.

Smedes, Lewis B. *Choices: Making Right Decisions in a Complex World.* San Francisco, CA. Harper & Row. 1986.

Smith, Huston, with Phil Cousineau. *And Live Rejoicing.* Novato, CA. New World Library. 2012.

Smith, Huston, with Phil Cousineau. *The Way Things Are.* Berkeley, CA. University of California Press. 2003.

Stutz, Phil and Barry Michaels. *The Tools.* New York, NY. Spiegel & Grau. 2012.

Tolstoy, Leo. *The Thoughts of Wise People for Every Day of the Year.* Richmond, Surrey, United Kingdom. Alma Books LTD. 2015.

Welch, David A. *Decisions, Decisions: The Art of Effective Decision Making.* Amherst, NY. Prometheus Books. 2002.

Wooden, John. *A Lifetime of Observations and Reflections, On and Off the Court.* New York, NY. McGraw Hill. 1997.

Woodward, Orrin. *Resolved, 13 Resolutions for LIFE.* Cary, NC. Obstacles Press. 2018.